WATERFALLS, FOUNTAINS, POOLS & STREAMS

WATERFALLS, FOUNTAINS, POOLS & STREAMS

Designing & Building Water Features in Your Garden

HELEN NASH & EAMONN HUGHES

Sterling Publishing Co., Inc.
New York

Designed by Judy Morgan

Library of Congress Cataloging-in-Publication Data

Nash, Helen, 1944-
 Waterfalls, fountains, pools & streams : designing & building
water features in your garden / Helen Nash & Eamonn Hughes.
  p. cm.
  Includes index.
  ISBN 0-8069-9665-X
  1. Water gardens-Design and construction. 2. Water in landscape
architecture. I. Hughes, Eamonn (Eamonn F.) II. Title.
SB423.N39 1997
624-dc21   97-22142
                                                                CIP

5   7   9   10   8   6   4

First paperback edition published in 1999 by
Sterling Publishing Company, Inc.
387 Park Avenue South, New York, N.Y. 10016
© 1998 by Helen Nash & Eamonn Hughes
Distributed in Canada by Sterling Publishing
% Canadian Manda Group, One Atlantic Avenue, Suite 105
Toronto, Ontario, Canada M6K 3E7
Distributed in Great Britain and Europe by Cassell PLC
Wellington House, 125 Strand, London WC2R 0BB, England
Distributed in Australia by Capricorn Link (Australia) Pty Ltd.
P.O. Box 704, Windsor, NSW 2756 Australia
Printed in Hong Kong
All rights reserved

Sterling ISBN 0-8069-9665-X Trade
0-8069-9666-8 Paper

Additional photo credits

page 2: Carol Christensen; page 3: H. Nash; page 5: Carol Christensen; pages 6-7: Carol Christensen; page 8: Carol
Christensen; page 10: Carol Christensen; page 11: Richard Schmitz; page 12: Carol Christensen; page 22: Carol
Christensen; page 34: Eamonn Hughes; page 60: Eamonn Hughes; page 74: Carol Christensen;
page 82: Gordon T. Ledbetter

For Carol Christensen,
whose eyes see the beauty and
whose camera captures the magic,
and for Kathy Hughes.

CONTENTS

INTRODUCTION

The 1995 Grand Award from the Associated Landscape Contractors of America went to Post Landscape Services in Atlanta, Georgia, for the design and installation of this stream, garden, and koi pond.

William Butler Yeats stood on the side of a street in London, far from the shore of his lakeside home in Ireland:

"I will arise and go now, for always night and day I hear lake water lapping with low sounds by the shore; While I stand on the roadway, or on the pavements grey, I hear it in the deep heart's core."

The vision of water captivates our senses, but as Yeats noted, the sound of water moves deep within our spirit. That sound may be but a gentle lapping, trickle, or riffle or it may be a magnificent crashing of water upon itself or rocks. Whichever, its sound speaks to elemental needs of the human spirit for life, peace, and harmony.

Incorporating that sound into our backyards and environment can take many forms—a simple fountain, a gurgling stream, a sheen of glass over a tumble of rocks, exotic tiers of glistening droplets, or water pouring from an earthen jar. With the movement of water, the stress of the day and anxieties of the spirit are carried away.

It is not necessary to retreat to a second home far from Thomas Gray's madding crowd. Your backyard can provide that solace and tranquility. While others may briefly enter your world to create that oasis, a great satisfaction results from creating it yourself.

I remember as a child my mother deciding on a project she wished to take care of around the house. She dragged my sister and me along with her to the public library, gathered every book on the subject to study rigorously, and subsequently did the work herself.

I remember my first pond: With little instruction then available in print, my husband Dave and I wrestled with a 100 × 50 foot liner to lay within an excavation meticulously leveled at each shelf layer—only to discover that it was the top edge of the pond that needed to be level. We rued the lack of accessible information!

Sterling Publishing requested this book for you. With monthly production of Water Gardening magazine, I knew I could not attend to the topic with the thoroughness I would demand myself. My standards remained the same: to provide solid, detailed information on how to do it yourself so the results will

be professional in quality and endurance. I needed expert help with this project! Only one name came to mind: Eamonn Hughes. Eamonn is a transplanted Irishman who learned his water-crafting trade from Gordon T. Ledbetter. With a gift for design and a knowledge of construction, Eamonn also possesses that rare "teacher mentality"—a willingness to share what he has learned to help others achieve the dream.

This book is a treasure-trove of practical information and inspiration. It was not enough simply to describe and show construction methods we have tried and tested over time. We decided it was equally important to include photos of constructions to provide design ideas to spur your imagination. Whether your dream is a simple interpretation of moving water or a glorious swelling of expansive waters, we wish to enable you to create in your yard what William Butler Yeats only recalled in spirit far from home. At the close of each of your days, may you enjoy the soul-satisfying peace of the waters within your own private gardens.

Helen Nash and
Eamonn Hughes

PLANNING

Water cascading gently through a rock waterfall satisfies sight and sound while maintaining conditions for growing aquatic plants.

Planning is the key to any successful project. To include moving water in your backyard, consider the following questions:

What atmosphere do you want to create? Whatever the landscape style of your private haven, water adds a psychological element that can ease the soul. Moving waters enhance a landscape visually and aurally. If your garden already offers you a relaxing respite from the world, the gentle babble and gurgle of a nearby stream or the soft patter of a fountain may be the crowning touch to your secret garden. The romantic garden, the wildlife garden, the Japanese garden, the formal garden—all find complementary beauty in softly flowing waters.

A surging mountain stream, a crashing waterfall, a thunderous fountain—these all nourish a zest for life. If your garden area is large enough to include a water feature at some distance from your house, you can approach and enjoy it in full splendor and also delight in it as background music while you contemplate your "other" garden closer to home.

The sound of water can mask the noise of traffic and the world beyond your haven. But consider the volume of sound you desire. Carefully selecting the site of a feature will provide a delightful sound from your patio or through the nighttime bedroom window. If you have neighbors close by, remember that they might not welcome the constant rushing of a Niagara Falls all night long.

How much time do you spend in the garden? Consider both your lifestyle and your climate. Working in the garden invites gentle, relaxing water sounds. More active waters encourage warm, convivial feelings and sociability. Visible and more audible features can be enjoyed from within a home.

In warmer climate zones, of course, you will have more time during the year to enjoy the fea-ture. In colder climates the time you can spend outside around a water feature is limited, and maintenance considerations, such as leaf-fall and freezing waters, arise.

Even if you don't have small children, consider who might visit or who live nearby. Youngsters are naturally attract-ed to water and plants and liv-ing creatures. Your planning must involve providing safety for young visitors. These accommodations might be a fence around the pond or adap-tations to the pond itself.

After considering all this, con-sider the cost. *How much can you afford to spend for your water feature?* Your budget determines how much of the project you can hire out, as well as how much of the project you can complete at a given time. Your dream water feature need not be modified to a lesser scale if it can be completed in stages—the reservoir pond the first year, a stream and/or waterfall the second year, and a header pond the third year, for example.

Designing Your Project

Your primary concern should be to make your design appro-priate to the style and design of your home. This sets a tone of inherent harmony in the pro-ject—formal or informal, large or small. Gather together mate-rials to survey your garden: a large sheet of graph paper; a ruler, yardstick, or tape mea-sure; pencil and eraser; a spirit level, and a long, straight board or a line level and lightweight

Part of the pleasure of a water feature in the yard involves enjoying it with friends.
Photo by Eamonn Hughes.

The best of both worlds may require a dual pond design to accommodate both water lilies and treasured koi. A waterfall connects the two ponds, with the water recycling from the fish pond below.

string; a suitable length of garden hose or rope; 10 to 20 short wooden stakes and a hammer; a note pad for field measurements; and a camera.

Measure the sides of the garden and the house and draw them onto the graph paper. If the garden is small, a 1:20 scale is adequate with one inch equal to 20 feet. To fit the design of a larger garden onto a piece of graph paper may require a 1:40 or a 1:50 scale. Measure where patios, decks, windows, and doors are located and site them on your plan. Note positions of large shrubs and trees as you mark North on your design to determine areas of full sun and shade. Note accessibility of services such as water and electricity.

Although eyeballing the terrain gives a general idea of its slope (such as basically flat, gently rolling, or steeply sloped), the success of your design of waterfalls and streams depends on available and created elevations. Conversely, an apparently flat yard that varies in elevation by only a few inches can disrupt a design that needs to be level. A builder's level and the straight board aid in plotting elevation changes in an area. In gently rolling terrain, for example, it is necessary to cut through some

Even a small pond can feature the gentle sound of moving water.

Photo by Carol Christensen.

of the slopes to maintain the level area of the pond and yet provide the downhill slope required for a stream and/or waterfall. A line level in which a string is stretched tightly between two points, the carpenter level suspended and the bubble centered, and the measurement taken from the string to the ground, works well over greater lengths. Stakes are pounded into the ground to indicate elevation differences around the site. A hired professional might use a two-man tripod level or a one-man laser level.

How you plan to enjoy the garden will determine the design layout. If you will view it primarily from inside the house or from a patio, plan for maximum visibility from there. Lay out garden hoses or lengths of rope to test visibility. Make frequent checks from vantage points and use the camera to determine the final siting. Once you are satisfied with the design, use lime or marking paint to outline its features on the ground. At this point, remind yourself that the one thing most pond owners later regret is the size of the finished pond; inevitably, people end up

Connecting two small ponds with a narrow, winding stream satisfies the desire for water in a garden of special plants.

Photo by Carol Christensen.

A simple raised pond achieves elegance with dramatic plantings and the frothy accent of a fountain. Photo by Carol Christensen.

wishing they had made their pond bigger.

Include in your plans all the necessary safety features. Plan a child-safe feature such as a cobbled reservoir pond, stream, or fountain if necessary. These designs look and sound great.

Computing the Cost of Your Project

Because building a concrete-formed structure requires expertise, consult with reputable professionals to determine the cost of this method of construction. Preformed or molded features limit the design possibilities, but they are easy to price. You will probably want to consider a sand cushion of two to four inches beneath the forms and around them, but you can

ignore costs such as underlay and pond membrane.

In most instances, the flexible membrane offers the greatest latitude in design, and is durable and long-lasting. Before deciding on a liner, compare strength, thickness, and composition. If fish are planned for the feature, the membrane should be non-toxic to them. Often the warranty indicates the expected life of the liner. A water feature is work to construct and costs money, but will provide years of enjoyment and will enhance the value of your home. Use quality materials from the beginning to protect your investment.

Make a list of the materials required to build your design. If possible, price the items from more than one source. Once you know approximately how

much it will cost to build your design, you can decide if you will build it all at once or in stages over more than one year. *If you build the project over several seasons, make your initial reservoir pond large enough to support the completed feature; a stream or waterfall added later can be sized to fit the reservoir pond, but the reservoir pond cannot be made larger without risk of leakage.* Use the following guidelines to determine quantities of materials required:

Computing Flexible Liner Requirements

There are two easy methods of computing liner size for your new pond. These are figured after you have excavated the pond's form. Lay a flexible tape measure loosely along the longest axis of the pond. Allow an extra six inches or so for securing the liner at the pond's edge. Repeat this process to obtain a measure of the width of the pond, too.

Another method is to pull a tape measure tightly across the widest part of the pond excavation and then again along the longest part. Note these measurements. Next, measure the greatest depth. Enter all these measurements into the following formula:

Maximum length + (2 × maximum depth) + 2' for overlap = total length of liner

Maximum width + (2 × maximum depth) + 2' for overlap = total width of liner

Total length of liner × total width of liner = total square feet of liner needed.

If you have a stream or waterfall flowing into your pond, follow this same computation process for each section of your project.

A tranquil stream winding through the property creates harmony in the landscape design.

Photo by Carol Christensen.

Computing the Project's Water Volume

Extensive waterfall systems and streams can result in disaster if they are not sized appropriately to the reservoir pond. Whatever water that runs through the system is drawn from the reservoir pond at its base. Enough water to fill the courseway must be pumped into the system before it can return to the pond. An improper size courseway can leave the pond lowered by several unsightly inches. Topping off the pond to make up for the removed water works only until the pump is turned off and the courseway waters drain back into the pond and flood the surrounding area. Use the following chart to determine the size reservoir or bottom pond needed to service the length courseway you envision having.

Computing Reservoir Pond Size Required for Waterfall/Stream

Water Drops in Reservoir Pond with Stream System
Note: Assume 3-inch depth of water in stream courseway and 3-foot width of stream.

Drops in inches when stream is designated by feet in length:

Reservoir Pond in feet	10'	15'	20'	25'	30'	40'	50'	75'	100'
4 x 4	3.9	5.6	7.8	9.8	11.7	15.63	19.53	29	39.06
4 x 5	3.13	4.69	6.25	7.8	9.38	12.5	15.63	23.44	37.5
4 x 6	2.6	3.9	5.21	6.5	7.8	10.42	13.02	19.532	6.04
4 x 7	2.23	3.35	4.46	5.6	6.7	8.93	11.16	16.74	22.32
4 x 8	1.95	2.93	3.9	4.89	5.90	7.81	9.77	14.65	22.06
5 x 5	2.5	3.75	5	6.25	7.5	10	12.5	18.75	30
5 x 6	2.08	3.13	4.17	5.2	6.25	8.33	10.42	15;.63	20.83
5 x 7	1.79	2.68	3.55	4.46	5.35	7.14	8.93	13.39	17.86
5 x 8	1.56	2.34	3.13	3.9	4.7	6.25	7.81	11.72	15.63
5 x 9	1.39	2.08	2.78	3.47	4.17	5.56	6.94	10.42	13.89
5 x 10	1.25	1.88	2.5	3.12	3.75	5	6.25	9.38	12.5
6 x 6	1.74	2.6	3.46	4.3	5.2	6.94	8.68	13.02	17.36
6 x 7	1.49	2.23	2.98	3.72	4.5	5.95	7.44	11.16	14.89
6 x 8	1.3	1.95	2.6	3.3	3.9	5.21	6.51	9.77	13.02
6 x 9	1.16	1.74	2.3	2.9	3.5	4.63	5.79	8.68	11.57
6 x 10	1.04	1.56	2.08	2.6	3.1	4.12	5.21	7.81	10.42
7 x 7	1.28	1.91	2.55	3.18	3.8	5.1	6.38	9.57	12.76
7 x 8	1.12	1.67	2.23	2.79	3.35	4.46	5.58	8.37	11.16
7 x 9	.99	1.49	1.98	2.48	2.97	3.97	4.96	7.44	9.92
7 x 10	.89	1.34	1.79	2.23	2.67	3.57	4.46	6.7	8.93
7 x 12	.74	1.12	1.49	1.86	2.23	2.98	3.73	5.58	7.44
7 x 14	.64	.96	1.28	1.59	1.91	2.55	3.19	4.78	6.38
8 x 8	.98	1.46	1.95	2.44	2.9	3.9	4.89	7.32	9.77
8 x 10	.78	1.17	1.56	1.95	2.34	3.13	3.91	5.86	7.81
8 x 12	.65	.98	1.3	1.63	1.95	2.6	3.26	4.88	6.51
8 x 14	.56	.84	1.12	1.39	1.67	2.23	2.79	4.19	5.58
8 x 16	.49	.73	.98	1.22	1.46	1.95	2.44	3.3	4.88
9 x 10	.69	1.04	1.39	1.74	2.08	2.78	3.47	5.21	6.94
9 x 12	.58	.87	1.16	1.45	1.74	2.31	2.89	4.34	5.79
9 x 14	.496	.74	.99	1.24	1.48	1.98	2.48	3.72	4.96
9 x 16	.43	.65	.87	1.09	1.17	1.74	2.17	3.26	4.34
9 x 18	.39	.58	.77	.96	1.16	1.54	1.93	2.89	3.86
10 x 10	.63	.94	1.25	1.56	1.88	2.5	3.13	4.69	6.25
10 x 12	.52	.78	1.04	1.3	1.56	2.08	2.6	3.9	5.36
10 x 14	.45	.67	.89	1.12	1.34	1.92	2.23	3.35	4.46
10 x 16	.39	.59	.78	.98	1.17	1.56	1.95	2.93	3.9
10 x 18	.35	.52	.69	.87	1.04	1.39	1.74	2.6	3.47
10 x 20	.31	.47	.63	.78	.94	1.25	1.56	2.34	3.13
12 x 15	.35	.52	.69	.87	1.04	1.39	1.74	2.6	3.47
12 x 24	.22	.33	.43	.54	.65	.87	1.04	1.65	2.17
15 x 20	.21	.31	.42	.52	.63	.83	1.04	1.56	2.08
15 x 25	.17	.23	.33	.42	.5	.67	.83	1.25	1.67
15 x 30	.14	.19	.28	.35	.42	.56	.69	1.04	1.39
20 x 25	.13	.17	.25	.31	.38	.45	.63	.94	1.25
20 x 30	.10	.14	.21	.26	.31	.42	.52	.78	1.04
20 x 40	.08	.11	.16	.195	.23	.31	.39	.59	.78

Lush foliage partially conceals the waterfall to create a magical sense of mystery.

Computing Quantities of Building Supplies

Concrete blocks are available in both solid and hollow forms in measurements of 4x8" wide or 4x10" long.

Crushed limestone or hardcore is sold by the ton. Also known as #53, one ton fills approximately 20 cubic feet.

Flagstone, slate, and flat granite are sold by the ton. Lighter weights of the stone up to 1.5 inches in thickness cover from 100 to 150 square feet, while heavier weights cover 70–80 square feet. Stone suppliers can give specific coverages for selected stone.

Ground cover aggregates and pea gravel are sold by the ton. Pebbles, nuggets, and chips are generally figured at 100 square feet of coverage at a depth of 2 inches or 150 square feet of coverage at a depth of 1.5 inches.

Mulch, in the form of shredded bark, is sold by the yard with one yard covering 100 square feet at a 3-inch depth.

Sand is sold by the ton. One ton is approximately 20 cubic feet.

Stone bark and crater rock ground cover aggregates cover approximately 225 square feet at a 2-inch depth per ton.

Topsoil, pulverized, is sold by the ton/yard with 1 ton equal to about 1 yard that covers 27 cubic feet.

Featherock boulders weigh approximately 64 pounds per cubic foot.

Granite boulders weigh approximately 200 pounds per cubic foot.

Marble boulders weigh approximately 150 pounds per cubic foot.

Brick is figured at 4.5 bricks per square foot, laid flat.

Cement and mortar, sold in 80-pound bags, premixed, fills 2 square feet at a 4-inch depth.

Cobbles or round stones that fit within two open hands are available at 30 to 35 per ton.

To determine how much concrete or mortar your project requires, multiply the thickness in inches desired by the length and by the width and divide by 12 to determine the number of cubic feet. Divide that figure by 27 to figure the number of cubic yards.

Moving water, koi, and aquatic plants—a pleasing combination.

Materials and Tools Required

Shovels

Pickax

Wheelbarrow

Line level (optional)

Spirit level and straightedge

Hacksaw

Wooden stakes

Hose

Garden rake

Mortar trowel

Rock for sides and waterfalls

River rock

Pond liner

Pump

Delivery hose or pipe

Adapter connections to attach delivery lines to pump

PVC glue (if using PVC pipes)

EPDM glue to glue down pleats in pond liner

Consider the proportions of your design. This feature combines a 12-foot cascade and a 15' × 6' and 18-inch-deep pond.

Photo by Eamonn Hughes.

Professional Help

If you decide to hire a qualified contractor or landscape architect to do the work for you, select this person as carefully as you would the person you would choose to design and build your home. Check the references supplied by the contractors you select to bid on the project. Talk to previous clients to assure yourself of the quality of work, timeliness of completion, work practices, and care of surrounding areas. Determine if any problems were handled quickly, efficiently, and fairly.

Check to see whether the contractor has any business licenses required in your locale. If the builder is licensed, check with the licensing authority to determine whether outstanding claims exist. Check that the company carries enough liability and employee insurance to cover any accidents that might happen on your site. Before you make your final decision, arrange to see some of the contractor's completed projects to be certain you are fully comfortable with the quality and style of construction.

A geyser water fountain set in the pond at a distance from the house makes for an attractive water feature.

Photo by Carol Christensen.

BASIC INSTALLATION

*A
ribbon
of water becomes
an enchanting
waterfall.*

Most of the water features discussed in the following chapters use basic installation practices: determining levels, excavating, setting liners, mixing and using mortar, moving and setting rocks. Refer to this chapter before performing these steps.

Determining Levels

Use your master plan or design to mark the ground where the excavation for your water feature will be. Use spray paint, builder's chalk, or cat litter to make the marks. Having already determined elevations in the area, now you must establish the level of the perimeter area of the project. The reservoir pond that water from the waterfall/stream recirculates through must be perfectly level around its edges to prevent the water level from appearing lopsided and out of kilter.

Most backyard pond reservoirs can be leveled with a builder's spirit level and a straightedge. A spirit level is a straightedge housing that

A paint spray gun marks the outline of the project before excavation.

Photo by Eamonn Hughes.

A small carpenter's spirit level determines levels from side to side of a narrow stream excavation. Photo by H. Nash.

way, determine the level of the water running through the channel within aesthetic proportions. For example, your design might call for one bank to be higher than the other, but generally opposite banks are within a small range of each other's level.

To establish levels with a builder's spirit level, pound a pointed stake into the ground 6 to 12 inches behind the pond or courseway edge. This first stake is called the *datum peg* and serves as the guide that all the others will match. The length of your straightedge determines how far apart you can site the stakes. Pound the next stake and each subsequent stake at a distance that allows the straightedge to rest upon the top of both pegs. Place the spirit level on the straightedge and adjust the new stake to the same level as the previous stake (to match that of the datum peg). After the stakes have been set all around the pond perimeter or along the water courseway, double-check them from the opposite direction and across the area.

For larger projects, a water level may be used. Inexpensive,

encloses a bubble within a liquid. When level, the bubble is centered in the liquid. If the level is too low or too high, the bubble will settle to one side or the other. A straightedge is a long, straight, smooth piece of lumber on which the builder's spirit level is placed. By resting the straightedge across the tops of wooden stakes, you can use a builder's spirit level to determine if the proposed construction is level.

In excavating a waterfall, the same principle is used, although the spirit level may be rested directly on the excavated steps of the courseway as well as on wooden stakes extending across the excavation, to assure level. Likewise, in laying out a course-

USING A CARPENTER'S SPIRIT LEVEL

Each stake is pounded in to be level with the preceding one. Double-check across the length and width of the pond by using a long straightedge and spirit level.

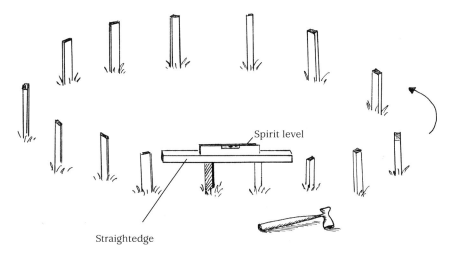

Spirit level

Straightedge

Using a Line Level

Stake one end of the string at ground level. Pull the string tightly and adjust its height until the bubble is centered in the level.

Photo by Eamonn Hughes.

Close-up of a line level.

Photo by Eamonn Hughes.

Use a felt-tipped pen to mark the elevation from the soil to the level.

Photo by Eamonn Hughes.

When the bubble is centered in the level, mark the stake with a felt-tipped pen.

Photo by Eamonn Hughes.

clear, hose-end attachments convert garden hoses for this use. A length of clear hosing may also be used. Pound in the datum peg to the desired level for the project. Fill the hose with water, taking care no air bubbles are within the water line. Tie one end of the hose firmly to the datum peg. Bring the other end of the hose up next to the datum peg, taking care not to spill any water from the hose or else you may need to restart the procedure. When the water level in the loose end of the hose agrees with the datum end, mark the water

By attaching clear hosing to the end of a garden hose, levels across larger excavations can be determined.

Photo by Eamonn Hughes.

THE HOSE LEVEL

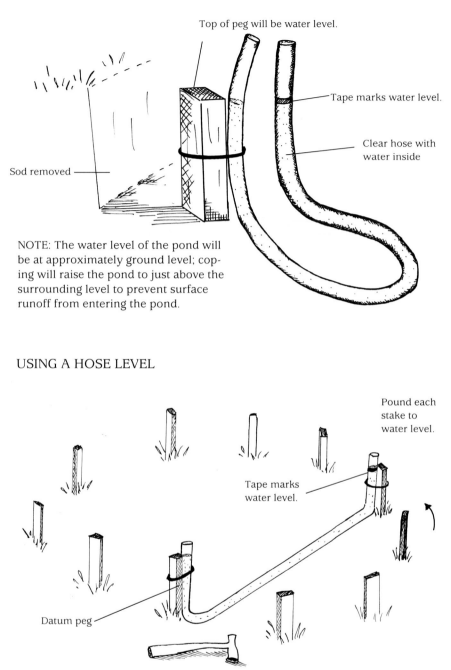

Top of peg will be water level.

Tape marks water level.

Clear hose with water inside

Sod removed

NOTE: The water level of the pond will be at approximately ground level; coping will raise the pond to just above the surrounding level to prevent surface runoff from entering the pond.

USING A HOSE LEVEL

Pound each stake to water level.

Tape marks water level.

Datum peg

A laser level can be operated by only one person. Photo by H. Nash.

level on the loose end with tape or a laundry pen. Carefully take the hose to each stake around the pond's perimeter and pound in the stakes until their top edges and the water in the hose agree.

Professional excavators frequently use a telescopic apparatus that requires the assistance of a second person. Laser levels can be operated by only one person. These levels are beneficial for determining level heights of large waterfall designs, especially those built into hillsides.

Excavation

Smaller ponds can be excavated by hand. Remove one shovel's depth at a time from the entire

Establishing Section Levels

Lay the level on the ground at what will be the source of the stream and pound in a peg at the other end of the level's reach. Mark the peg with a felt-tipped pen to show the elevation drop. Photo by Eamonn Hughes.

Place one end of the level on the mark on the first peg and repeat the process. Photo by Eamonn Hughes.

Place one end of the level on the mark on peg number 2 and pound in a third stake. Mark the level as before. Photo by Eamonn Hughes.

pond area. Cleanup is made easier by putting the excavated soil or "spoil" on a nearby tarp. If a shelf is to be constructed within the pond, mark the shelf edge with spray paint once the desired depth is obtained. Usually shelves will be only a foot deep and at least a foot wide. The excavation then proceeds in the same manner to

having to install a bottom drain. Should the pond construction be in a high-water-table area, you may wish to provide in-ground drainage pipes either across the bottom of the excavation or around it to direct ground water away and prevent it from causing the liner to bubble up.

Waterfall excavation into exist-

Larger excavations may be expedited with the use of professional equipment. Photo by Eamonn Hughes.

the bottom.

Except for construction of larger natural ponds with gently sloped sides, most ponds should have nearly vertical sides to better conceal the pond liner and to allow easy access to the pond. Provide a sump area in the pond bottom to facilitate pond drainage and to avoid

Smaller excavations can be carved out by hand shovels.

Photo by Eamonn Hughes.

ing or well-tamped soil essentially carves out a stairway. Be sure to provide enough depth to the stepped excavation to accommodate the rocks and stones you will use.

Stream courses are a variation of waterfall construction. They may include a short series of falls, occasional small pond or bog areas, or winding riffles of running water. The stream may be excavated as a stretch of gradually lowering elevation into the reservoir pond from which its water recycles, or it may be excavated as a series of level sections that are connected to lower areas via short falls.

Setting the Liner

Be sure the excavation is free of sharp stones or protruding roots that could puncture the liner when the weight of the water bears upon it. Fabric underlay, a thick layer of newspapers, and/or a layer of sand helps protect the liner. Fit the liner into the shell, making folds and pleats as needed. Be sure enough excess extends beyond the top of the excavation to help form a barrier to prevent surface runoff from entering the pond.

Waterfalls and courseways should also be fully lined. Since they involve a flow of water from a higher elevation into the lower pond reservoir, it is not

The small project may be lined with a single piece of membrane.
Photo by Eamonn Hughes.

Larger projects work best with the waterfall or stream lined separately from the reservoir pond. Photo by Eamonn Hughes.

necessary that their liner be of one piece with the bottom pond's. As long as the liner section from the higher elevation overlaps the lower section, leaks will not occur. With courseway sections, the same principle of overlapping liner sections into lower elevations applies. While any folds or pleats may be glued flat, fold them so water flows over the crease rather than into the fold. Try to avoid positioning the fold where it will be visible.

Mixing Mortar

Concrete is made of specific amounts of cement, sand, gravel, and water. Mortar is similar but has no gravel in the mix. Both may be purchased premixed in 80-pound bags. Each makes up ⅔ cubic foot. Water is the catalyst that causes the material to harden; the less water, the stronger the mix and the stiffer and more difficult it is to work. You may use mortar to set stonework around the pond edge as well as in the waterfall and courseway. Concrete may be used to create solid pads that stabilize large rockwork in the waterfall or courseway. Concrete support pads are also built beneath the liner to support heavy rockwork set upon the liner or fountain plinth constructions.

Weather is a critical factor; freezing conditions invite disintegration of the concrete before it has cured, and very hot conditions may allow it to dry too quickly, also resulting in a weak and disintegrating product. If stone aggregate is mixed into the concrete or mortar, the stone must be clean to ensure a good bond. The water used in the mix must also be very clean.

Particularly in areas where the ground freezes, concrete and mortar are susceptible to cracking. Hence, it is very important that portions of the water feature's design that use mortared stonework be lined beneath with a waterproof membrane. Support pads subject to such weather should be of sufficient thickness to lessen disintegration. When the concrete must be more than four inches thick, hardware screen or rebar between the layers of poured concrete is recommended. Be certain, however, that reinforcing metals do not protrude from the concrete, press on the liner, or create leaks. In the case of hot weather combined with clay soil, a layer of crushed stone around the concrete pad helps prevent ground shrinkage from cracking the support base. A formula for foundation and footing concrete is 1 part cement to 2 parts sharp sand to 4 parts aggregate.

Mortar lacks the strength of concrete since the stone aggregate is missing. Mortar is used to embed stonework and create seals between stones. It is not an all-purpose glue. Masonry mortar has a bit more flexibility than regular mortar mixes; it contains lime, which helps the mix resist cracking from temperature changes. While mortar comes premixed in 80-pound bags, it is less expensive to mix your own if large quantities are to be used. A standard mortar mix is 1 part lime, 2 parts portland cement, and 9 parts sharp sand. A simple measure is a shovelful. Thoroughly dry-mix the ingredients with a hoe or shovel before adding water. A large wheelbarrow is a convenient mixing container. Add water a bit at a time and mix with the hoe. The mortar should stand in peaks and create suction when a trowel is wiggled flat into it. If the mix is too thin, it will run; if it is too thick, it will not bond well.

Stop adding water just before you think it is enough to avoid a runny mix. Should the mix be runny, add more premix or more cement and sand. You can also let the mix rest for half an hour to allow the water to rise to the surface and then carefully pour it off. If the mixture is not too runny, wait until the water starts to rise to the surface and begin working with the stiffer mortar from the bottom of the mix.

Generally, in working with stone, spread a one-inch-thick layer of mortar, and rock the stone firmly into place. This pushes out some of the mortar, which is then trimmed with the trowel. In working with bricks, cover the end edges with mortar before placing them on a thin layer of mortar.

To mortar a joint from the outside after the stone or brick is in place, put a little mortar on the bottom edge of the trowel, near the tip, and smear it into the crevice with a push-and-wipe action. This is called "pointing up." Mortar should be recessed so the stones appear to be jutting naturally from the ground. Recessing can be performed up to 12 hours after the work has been done. Use a wire brush to scrub the crumbly surface mortar.

Curing both mortar and cement allows the chemical action to be completed. The work should be kept moist for up to six days. Cover the area with plastic sheets or wet burlap. Once the mortar or concrete has set and will not wash or run out, moisten it with a hose twice a day, or more frequently in hot weather.

Even the neatest mortaring job may leave stains and smears on the rocks. Much of this can be removed during the crumbly stage of curing with a wire brush. Stubborn stains can be removed with a solution of 1 part muriatic acid to 10 parts water. Be sure to run ample water over the cleaned work to avoid any trace of the acid or lime from the mortar/concrete affecting the water pH—either condition of which may jeopardize your fish.

Moving Heavy Rocks

Avoid back strain and injury by moving heavy rocks sensibly. In lifting smaller ones, squat down and rise from the knees, back straight, rather than bending over from a standing position. Wear a sportsman's back brace for extra support.

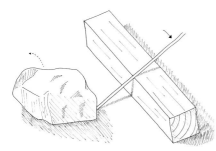

Push lever down to move rock.

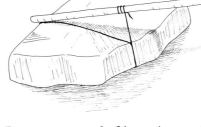

Pressure on end of lever is created by pulling lever up.

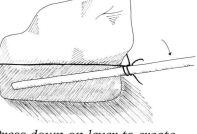

Press down on lever to create upward pressure against rock.

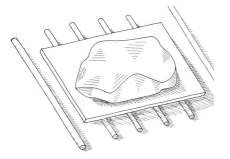

As platform slides over rods, move freed rod to front.

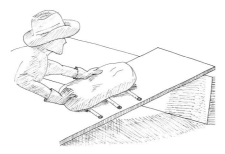

Combine a plank and rods to attain elevations.

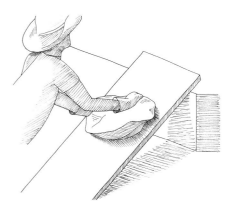

Roll rock end-over-end up a plank.

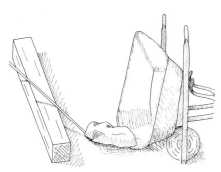

Leverage rock into a wheelbarrow.

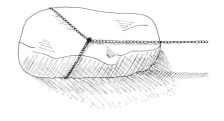

Chain or heavy rope can pull a rock from above or below.

Setting Rocks

Rocks up to two hundred pounds in weight can be maneuvered into place by hand. Larger rocks require the use of some form of equipment to avoid risking serious injury. How you set the rocks in the water course determines the finished effect. A finished section of rockwork that appears to jar the senses has usually been set with no thought of the rocks' natural strata and angles. Your water course should look as though it has been carved out of the bedrock by the flowing of the stream over hundreds of years. To achieve this illusion, study the form or shape of the rock. If it is an angular, blocky rock, decide on a plane or level—either horizontal or set at an angle. Set *all* the rocks at the same plane or angle. Your composition will then imitate nature rather than a rock slide.

A technique called "back mortaring" is very effective in achieving a natural look. Lay a two-inch-thick bed of mortar along the edge of the stream or waterfall. Gently press a rock into this bed and use a trowel to smooth mortar up against the back of the rock. Continue setting rock into this first layer. When the mortar in the first course has hardened enough to support weight, place another bed of mortar along the back edge of the top of the first course. Lay the rock into this second bed just as you did on the first. Vary the sizes of rock as much as possible to avoid a wall-like effect. When all the side walls are constructed, build the waterfall sections across the water course using the same technique. Cover the water course with graded river rock to complete the bed.

Study these examples for guidance in setting rocks naturally. Each project is completed with the "back mortaring" technique.

All photos by Eamonn Hughes.

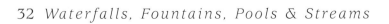

chapter three

WATERFALLS

Carved into a hillside, this Eamonn Hughes design was featured on the cover of the premier issue of Water Gardening magazine.

Plan for Success

Your waterfall is your signature. Its unique interpretation sets it apart from any other. To ensure success, follow these basic guidelines. See Chapter Two for additional construction guides.

Fully line your waterfall. Water inevitably finds a way to seep back into the structure and between rocks and stone. Unlined, with no way to channel that water *back* into the reservoir pond, the water level in the pond below will drop—the result of a mysterious leak. Ponds are recognized as a conservative use of water in the garden, but such a leak may be not only unsightly, it will also be costly and a waste of precious water. Should you notice an abnormal drop in the reservoir pond's level, turn off the waterfall pump and note whether the water loss stops or continues. If it stops, the leak is within the waterfall system. If it continues, check the reservoir pond itself for the problem.

Steve Wagner creates interest and sound with his waterfall design. Photo by Carol Christensen.

The waterfalls we create in our backyards derive inspiration from nature, for example, from the frothy upper falls of the Wild Columbine. Photo by Ron Everhart.

Less than a foot wide, Pat Slayter's weir creates a miniature mirror fall into his lower pond. Photo by Ron Everhart.

A wide weir creates a mirror fall at the Houston Museum of Art.

Photo by Anita Nelson.

Water rushes down a stone staircase at Longwood Gardens in Pennsylvania. Photo by H. Nash.

Cla Allgood combines the mirror-producing weir tucked within a wall with a stair-step cascade in this unique waterfall interpretation. Photo by Cla Allgood.

The Hewitt family's waterfall triple tier fall splits the mirror falls with precise placement of small stones at the edge of the spillway. Photo by Carole Taylor Reimer.

Naturally, it is preferable to use a single piece of liner for the entire waterfall construction. However, if the drop from one level to another is at least two or three inches above the lower level, overlapping a piece from above will not allow leakage. (This portion or *face* of the falls will be concealed and held in place by rockwork.) The liner from the lowest level of the waterfall should also overlap the pond liner by several inches. If you are not covering the face with rockwork, use EPDM glue to attach the overlap to the pond liner to prevent it from floating up in the water and showing.

Because a curve, especially near the top, creates the illusion of more water coming from a mysterious source, you may need to fold or pleat the liner in places to make it assume the courseway's shape. All folds should be in the same direction the water flows to prevent the folds from being pulled up through the river rock and exposed. Large folds may be glued together to make fitting stonework into the water run easier. The liner *must* extend above the water level at all points along the water course.

Plan your waterfall excavation to be wide enough and deep enough to accommodate whatever stonework you will use. Rocks look peculiar sitting on top of the ground, especially on a slope in a waterfall design. Rocks should look embedded into the ground. Excavate deeply into the slope and plan the water course with enough depth to accommodate both the water flow and the splash. If your waterfall is a trickle or is slow-moving, splash may not be a concern. However, little drops of water add up to a visible water loss. Generally, a four-inch-high channel *above* the anticipated water level is sufficient.

Consider the use of the pond area surrounding the water entry point. Water lilies do not like water movement or persistent splashing. If you plan to

If you wish to grow aquatic plants near your waterfall, plan for a gentle inflow into the pond.
Photo by Greg Jones.

Gently flowing waters between two connecting ponds allow full use of the water area for aquatics and water lilies. Photo by H. Nash

include these serene beauties in the area near your waterfall entry, the water must enter *gently*. You may wish to design your waterfall so its noise is created farther up the system rather than at the entry point. A wider lip (weir) at the entry point or a wide basin pond dissipates the force of the water flow.

Consider ground settling. Waterfalls constructed into the mounded pond excavation may settle in time and disrupt the water level and its flow. Mounded soil may settle to about half its loose mass over time. Ideally, the soil mounded for waterfalls and streams should not only be tamped down as much as possible, but it should be allowed to settle on its own over a period of time— as much as an entire season. (This provides a rationale for constructing the project in two stages.)

Another factor of ground settling is the weight of the rock-

How much under support is needed depends on your climate zone, soil type, and its state of compaction. Photo by H. Nash.

A stair-step structure in which the rocks do not weigh on each other may require little or no under support. Photo by H. Nash.

work used in the feature. A stream construction that incorporates waterfalls will be spread over a greater area. A waterfall constructed at the pond's edge involves stacking a considerable amount of heavy stone. Since the stacking proceeds to the *back* of the falls, the heaviest weight will rest there and will result in a disproportionate settling of the structure to a backward tilt. Supplying enough concrete support beneath the stonework avoids this problem. As a general rule, rocks weighing less than 200 pounds need only well-compacted soil or a generous layer of packed, crushed stone for support. Rocks weighing more than 200 pounds should have at least a 4-inch-thick concrete pad

beneath them if the soil tends to be soft and unstable. Even heavier rocks may require that the concrete pad be reinforced with mechanic's screen or rebar. In general, make the footing support equal to one-third the height of the structure.

Consider design basics. Your waterfall should fit naturally within the design of your pond, the overall landscape, and the design of your home. Maintaining consistent design makes your final product feel right and avoids jarring the senses. Likewise, the informal waterfall should nestle into its surroundings as opposed to jutting up starkly from the ground. If you wish to create elevation from the soil excavated from the pond, blend its mound into the surrounding terrain with a mixture of evergreen and deciduous shrubs.

In the same vein, consider the proportion of your waterfall as it relates to the reservoir pond and the overall landscape. A low waterfall with a very wide

A steep hillside is an opportunity for a natural waterfall.

Photo by Eamonn Hughes.

The small, cozy garden is informally graced by a pond and waterfall. Photo by Carol Christensen.

A formal stair-step waterfall carries out the design of this Moorish pond in Phoenix.

Photo by Charles Henne.

Japanese-style gardens make exquisite use of plants, rocks, and water.

Photo by Marsha Alley.

though slightly more expensive, it is well worth the benefits.

The longer the water drop from one level to the next, the more likely the water will be drawn back to the face of the structure. This is a function of centrifugal force. To prevent the resulting "wet wall" appearance, keep the tiers of the waterfall close together or compensate with a more powerful water flow. A stronger flow can be achieved with either a more powerful pump or by providing enough space from the water's entry at the same level as its exit to the next level, essentially by providing a length of run to allow a gain of speed. The berm rock over which the water exits to the next lower level should extend out from the face of the structure by at least two inches.

weir becomes a canal and loses its impact as a fall. A very large mound of rocks perched beside a very small pond feels uncomfortable and overpowering.

Consider basic scientific principles as you design the structure. Water is being pumped uphill to reach the top of the waterfall; for every foot of height from the pump, pumping capacity decreases. Manufacturers' charts take into account these reductions in lifting capacity. (See Chapter Five.) Likewise, resistance becomes a factor *within* the water line; for every ten feet of piping you must add another foot in lift height. Elbow turns within the water line reduce this even more. Avoid right-angle turns in the pipe if at all possible. Now

available is reinforced flexible tubing that reduces friction loss and delivers more water than a rigid pipe with elbows. Al-

Each section of a waterfall complex must be kept at the same level.

Photo by Richard Schmitz.

Waterfalls constructed in sections of short runs should be at the same level at both entry and exit. The excavation is deepened prior to the exit point to allow enough water to accumulate to spill over the berm.

While edge rocks can be dry-stacked along the water course, they need to be mortared in place at the spillway to force the water over the top. Do not use loose pea gravel in the streambed. The water flow will wash away sections and expose areas of the liner. The best material for a streambed is graded river rock, which varies in size from ¼" through 2". If the streambed is large, add 3–4" river rock into the mix to keep the size ratios appropriate.

A cobbled front must be mortared together to prevent the water from going back into the structure. Photo by H. Nash.

Construction Methods

There is more than one way to build a waterfall. The simplest waterfall may be little more than a short stacking of stones at the water's edge. More extensive waterfalls and courseways create options in construction method.

The **carved** construction method sculpts the waterfall into a mound or slope of soil.

Whether performed by an artful excavator or by hand, if the soil is firm enough, the entire base excavation can be literally carved into the existing soil.

Photo by Eamonn Hughes.

Mark on the excavation where you might further refine the sculpting. Photo by Eamonn Hughes.

In its raw form, it appears as a staircase leading to the pond's edge. The sculpted excavation is dug to accommodate the rockwork that will form the completed water course. If the course is sculpted into mounded soil from the pond excavation, be sure to tamp the soil well as you build the mound so you will not have problems later on with soil settling.

The **formed framework** construction method is especially useful in non-compacted soil and with sizable constructions in order to avoid massive stonework and its related expense. The method involves

Although fitting the small-to-medium-size pond, a stack of rocks can be heavy enough to merit building it upon a concrete support pad. Photo by Dave Artz.

the combination of both sculpting an excavation and building a framework of concrete blocks, which is then lined with a membrane and faced with rockwork. The facing may be bricks (as in a formal design), cobbles and larger stones, very large boulders, or "fake" rocks formed and carved of concrete facing. This construction method is easy to level, but it requires a large enough excavation to accommodate the blocks of the framework and the selected facing stone.

Variations in Waterfall Design

Your waterfall can be what you want it to be, visually, aurally, and functionally. As you design your project, consider the following suggestions: Create mystery and interest. A sense of mystery enhances the magic of your creation. Where is the water coming from? Whether you create a straightforward delivery from the top of a stack of rocks or a hidden spring around a bend, you will likely camouflage the water's entry at the top with rockwork or a small basin that empties the water down its run. If your waterfall mound is worked into the surrounding landscape, you have ample room to create mystery. Curve the water's pathway toward its top to create the illusion the water flows from a secret source an unknown distance away. Use large boulders or landscape specimens to partially conceal the water's run. These two techniques create more than mystery and interest;

they create *different* views from alternate vantage points. An element of surprise enhances your enjoyment of the feature.

Vary the water's flow through its course. Envision your construction as three areas: the top, the main courseway, and the entry. Water enters the design from a camouflaged or concealed source, often into a small reservoir or header pond. The water can then flow over the edges of sharp-edged rocks in mirror sheets of varying heights. (Note that a groove carved just inside the under edge of the stone prevents water from drawing back to the structure's face.) The elevation changes need not be of the same style. Alternate the mirror flows with cobbled drops that are simply steep slopes from one elevation to another, faced with large

Multiple ponds are connected by a variety of waterfalls.

Photo by Carol Christensen.

Combine heights of waterfall drops to incorporate elevation changes in the landscape.
Photo by H. Nash.

Large boulders create substance for the water. Photo by Eamonn Hughes.

Splitting a narrow waterfall into two paths creates interest.

Photo by Eamonn Hughes.

While on a grand scale, the principle provides inspiration—contrast a mirror fall with alternating levels of a cobbled and riffled fall. Photo by Anita Nelson.

Using a tee connection at the water outlet allows the water to be spread across a broader structure. Photo by Anita Nelson.

cobbles of stone or river rock to produce effects from rushes to gurgling riffles, depending on the rate of flow through the design. Split the flow with large rocks, boulders, or cobbles set within the courseway. As water flows around these interruptions, its force increases and both movement and sound are enhanced. Zigzag your courseway across the mound to create the illusion of a more expansive area.

Make planting areas within the waterfall itself. Rock garden planting methods of crevice and pocket planting create spots of interest in the structure. Also, a few aquatic plants will grow or thrive within the flowing waters. The most obvious plant is watercress or bittercress, often found growing in running streams and ditches in the wild, *Nasturtium officinale,* or *Cardamine cordifolia.* This plant thrives anchored only in gravel, but the bittercress form attains a rangy, bushy growth to nearly two feet in height. If the waterfall is large enough, watercress offers camouflage of portions of the water's flow and at the same time gives you delicious salad greens. Bog-type plants such as water iris, some rushes, arrowhead, pickerel weed, and water forget-me-not accept water's movement at the edge of the courseway. Expand the water's run to include a bog plant area that entertains accessible water out of the direct flow. (See Appendix for plant list.)

Incorporate vegetative filtration within the system. If the

Special preformed units are available for growing water clarifying aquatics. Photo by H. Nash.

water is gentle, design a bog pond somewhere along its path to use as vegetative filtration. This can be as simple as a widened area in the falls' courseway. Within your pond,

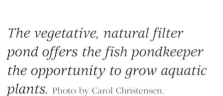

The vegetative, natural filter pond offers the fish pondkeeper the opportunity to grow aquatic plants. Photo by Carol Christensen.

A preformed pond, framed in stone, is juxtaposed with a larger reservoir pond to aid in water clarification through the use of plants. Photo by H. Nash.

Koi pondkeepers can enjoy a two-pond setup with the upper vegetative pond allowing the enjoyment of both aquatic plants and koi.

Photo by Carol Christensen.

the nitrogen cycle works to produce nitrates that feed murky-water-producing algae. Provide aquatic plants to absorb those nutrients and gain clearer water as well as more opportunity to enjoy the life within your pond. **Invite birds to enjoy the water.** Birds are naturally attracted to flowing water. So long as the flow is gentle, many neighborhood visitors will come to drink and bathe. Encourage these delightful visits with inviting conditions. Widen part of the courseway to include a pea-gravel beach area that allows easy access for the feathered ones. Birds will venture only where they can *see* that the water depth allows their wading. This need not be a great area; a slight widening of the streambed can accommodate a very small area welcomed by birds. Provide an open shrub or

driftwood perch for birds to preen on after bathing. You may be surprised to see that not only will the birds visit to partake of the water, but they may also relish tasty morsels of aquatic insects attracted by your water feature. Watercress, we have observed, seems to attract tasty insects that satisfy hungry visitors.

Incorporate a bio-filter within the system. Pondkeepers who choose to keep more fish than the minimal level commonly suggested of no more than one inch of goldfish per square foot of water surface or per 5 gallons of water volume often use a bio-filter to assist in converting ammonia produced by fish into nitrite and then into harmless nitrate. The waterfall system offers an ideal setup for bio-filters. Water flows from the pond to the bio-filter and then into

Bio-filter units may be set up at the rear of a waterfall to allow the water to filter through them before the routing back to the pond. Photo by H. Nash.

the waterfall for pond return. Excavate a space at the top of the waterfall behind the water's entry point to install a separate bio-filter system. Bio-filters can also be formed within the header pond at the top of the waterfall. Fill the shallow pond construction with appropriate media to invite colonies of beneficial bacteria that thrive in the presence of the oxygen-rich waters flowing through. These setups require slow-moving water of no greater than two gallons per minute per square foot of filter surface. A rule of thumb is to estimate 100 GPH per square foot of filter media. In figuring the amount of media surface, consider only the media exposed to flowing water.

As you consider these variations on the basic waterfall, remember that what you create is more than a mere rush or a trickle of recycled water. Your waterfall can be all things to you—a soul-satisfying sight and sound, an invitation to treasured feathered friends, an expansion of aquatic-plant-growing opportunities, an enhancement of clear pond waters, and an aid in better water quality for your finned pets.

The Stacked Rock Waterfall

The simple, stacked rock waterfall entry into the pond is appropriate for recycling water in the very small pond. Flat stones, usually the same as those used in the pond edging, are stacked to create a layer for a cascading re-entry of the recycled water. Flow is usually quite gentle—a trickle or gentle flow into the pond.

Slightly tilt the flagstone-type stone toward the pond to ensure water return. While mortar is not usually used in these constructions, mortar placed on the back half of the rocks helps prevent water loss and stabilizes the structure. If the construction extends back beyond the pond edge and liner enclosure, line it to ensure all water returns to the pond. Carve a groove perhaps one half inch in from the edge of the spillway stone on its *underside* to prevent water from drawing back. Water then

A stacking of flagstone pavers conceals the water entry for this simple waterfall.

Photo by Oliver Jackson.

falls cleanly back into the pond.

Stone selected for this construction should be hard and not subject to disintegration. Very hard rock, such as granite, takes considerable time to age and is not likely to produce an aged look. Many sources advise against using limestone for fear of altering pond water pH.

A very small submersible pump recycles water through this small feature. Photo by H. Nash

However, we have found that the use of limestone does little more than produce beneficial buffering of the water. Joe B. Dekker of The Waterscaping Company in New Jersey, for example, has lined the full bottom of his constructions with limestone to no ill effect for over 30 years. However, for your own peace of mind you may elect to monitor pond water pH with limestone use.

Tucked into a corner of the yard, a small preformed pool includes a simple waterfall by recycling the pond water through the stacked pavers. Photo by Oliver Jackson.

With a depression carved into a large stone, water is collected in the reservoir hidden by the decorative base stones to recycle through the simple but elegant feature. Photo by H. Nash.

The trickling sound of water emanates from this small waterfall that allows its enjoyment without concern of endangering young children. Photo by T.J. Smith.

Waterfalls need not be tall struc-tures to use the tee connection to split the flow of water.

Photo by Carol Christensen.

Elegant simplicity results in a Post Landscape design of water recycled over a single stone on its way through a man-made stream into a man-made lake.

Photo by Carol Christensen.

Carved or Sculpted Construction

This construction method works best on virgin soil on the side of a hill. It can be used also with mounded soil that is well tamped or provided with suitable under-reinforcement. Before sculpting the form, bring in the supply of stone you will use to line the excavation. Your sculpted, stair-step excavation must contain both the size and thickness of its lining rocks as well as suitable height on the side to confine any splash.

Carve the excavation into the mound or hillside. Use a single piece of liner, if possible, to overlap into the reservoir pond at the bottom. Glue the overlap-

A preformed unit known as a trough pond features a trickle of water to delight and refresh. Photo by Carol Christensen.

A stone to flow over and a stone to hide the water entry point equals a charming waterfall.

Photo by Ron Everhart.

ping flap to the pond liner with EPDM adhesive if the flap will not be held to the face by rock-work. With steep elevations, it is not necessary to check level and elevations of the total project. You do, however, want to be sure that the side-to-side elevations are level for a visually pleasing flow through the system. Any lengths of sections between drops in elevation should also be checked for level. (See Chapter Two.)

Begin at the bottom where the water re-enters the pond and work your way up the waterfall. Occasionally run water from a hose down your construction to

be sure the water will flow as you envision. Mortar the rocks into place as you proceed up the waterfall, working from the outside edge to first build the course's confining "walls." Bring the liner up above the projected water level on each side at least four inches to prevent potential water loss. (See Chapter Two for "mortar backlay" technique of construction.)

If you will vary your construction with mirror or cobbled falls, bog garden or mini-pond areas, or other variations, check those construction procedures and incorporate them as you work.

Stair steps are carved into the hillside. Each step is checked for level as it is sculpted, to ensure the water's flow per the design plans. Photo by Eamonn Hughes.

A single piece of EPDM rubber membrane is rolled down the hill to cover the excavation.

Photo by Eamonn Hughes.

Smaller projects are constructed in the same manner, but may not require so many helpers to adjust the liner over the entire project. Photo by Eamonn Hughes.

Cranes are used to move the massive boulders into position within the structure.

Photo by Eamonn Hughes.

Once the largest rocks have been set into place, the sides of the courseway are constructed by beginning with a bed of mortar.

Photo by Eamonn Hughes.

Set the base rock into the mortar. Photo by Eamonn Hughes.

Building up the mortar behind and upon the base rock, another rock is fit into place.

Photo by Eamonn Hughes.

Like piecing a three-dimensional puzzle, rocks are fitted together with mortar to create the form of the waterfall structure.

Photo by Eamonn Hughes.

Note as the work proceeds up the hill that the liner membrane extends beyond the framework of the structure.

Photo by Eamonn Hughes.

Before mortaring in the waterfall spillway rocks, lay them out dry to check for size and appearance. Photo by Eamonn Hughes.

The completed waterfall.

Photo by Eamonn Hughes.

Fake Rock Construction

The face of a hillside is sculpted, the pond and waterfall membrane draped over the entire structure, and chicken-wire mesh covers the area that will be turned into a rock wall. Gunnite is sprayed onto the wall, the chicken mesh providing a base form to secure it.

Photo by Eamonn Hughes.

Once the gunnite has been sprayed onto the surface, it awaits definition.

Photo by Eamonn Hughes.

The gunnite rock face is carved into a semblance of massive stone. Photo by Eamonn Hughes.

By studying real rocks, you can imitate their form and strata in your design.

Photo by Eamonn Hughes.

After the carving is completed, latex stains artificially age the appearance of the rockface.

Photo by Eamonn Hughes.

The completed waterfall of "fake rocks."

Photo by Eamonn Hughes.

Formed Framework Construction

This method is especially economical in cases of large waterfall constructions that might require a costly supply of stone. It is also useful with mounded soil that may not be settled enough to support long-term heavy construction.

Smaller projects built on established soils may use even a simple wood or landscape edging form. Larger and more elaborate courseways benefit from concrete block base structures. In all cases, closely observe levels as necessary! (See Chapter Two.)

As you excavate and construct the waterfall, allow room for the rock facing that will conceal the base structure.

An alternative construction useful in the larger project is to use the carved excavation or the preformed construction base as the form for "fake rocks" carved in concrete. Concrete or gunnite is sprayed onto a mesh-wire-covered form that is then molded and carved with knives and tools to appear to be massive stone boulders. The same technique performed manually forms the base structure with chicken wire shaped around tied rebar reinforcement. Smear and smooth concrete over the form, and then use knives to create rock grains and shape. Add dye to the concrete or paint the finished product with fish-safe paint to resemble real rock. Visit a public zoo for ideas on the use of this technique. While a major project, it can be highly fulfilling. Be certain, however, that this technique is compatible with your landscape and terrain.

Black plastic preformed waterfall courseways are concealed with stacked stone in a deck construction. Photo by H. Nash.

Preformed units may be found at local nursery suppliers.

Photo by Anita Nelson.

Stability is given the preformed waterfall by a concrete slab.

Photo by Anita Nelson.

Preformed Units, Tabletops, and Containers

Jim Sullivan uses real aquatic plant leaves as models for his sculpted waterfalls. Photo courtesy of Living Fountains.

A small in-deck pond recycles water through a carved feather rock waterfall. Photo by Greg Maxwell.

A desktop waterfall is sculpted of copper lotus leaves.

Photo by H. Nash.

A child-safe patio pond that uses a grate to support clay media in which plants are grown hydroponically features a carved feather rock waterfall Photo by H. Nash.

Creative Waterfall Interpretations

The Hoffmans' in-deck pond features an L-shaped tiered waterfall construction. Photo by Ron Everhart.

Cla Allgood interprets a variation of the wall-faced waterfall.
Photo by Cla Allgood.

A variation on the small-space waterfall features narrow streams of water falling from the wall. Photo by Anita Nelson.

Carved into a slight elevation around a raised planter, a two-tiered waterfall offers sound and visual delight. Photo by Eamonn Hughes.

A cobbled low-maintenance design features three small basin ponds that cascade water into the pond below.

Photo by Greg Jones.

Stepping-stones follow the curved weir of Gordon Ledbetter's natural pond design.

Photo by Gordon T. Ledbetter.

Meandering, semi-formal canals at the Dial Corporate Center are accented with water flowing down the brick-faced retaining wall.

Photo by Charles Henne.

Sean MacMamon designed rotating paddles to prevent fish from jumping the weir and escaping downstream.

Photo by Gordon T. Ledbetter.

A piano waterfall carries out the musical motif design.

Photo by Ron Everhart.

At the Royal Botanic Garden in Ontario, the Discovery waterfall demonstrates the movement of water in a unique design.

Photo by H. Nash.

The lines of the formal stair-step waterfall are repeated in planting beds in this hillside.

Photo by Anita Nelson.

STREAMS

A stream need not be expansive; tiny rivulets offer magical sight and sound.

Often, the pond is only the beginning, an open door to an endless possibility of magic created in your own backyard. Waterfalls add movement to pond designs, but what if you extend the water course-way? What if you turn it into a stream? Winding through the yard, a gentle ripple of water invites sound and design. Whether the stream is created in the larger landscape to appear fully natural or whether it is miniaturized in a smaller, confined space, you can still follow nature's guidelines: valleys, outcroppings, narrow channels, calm pools, gentle twists and turns, cobbled bedding, small falls, riffles and eddies, surging waters, and murmuring whispers. All can be duplicated to be in proportion to your pond and existing landscape.

Plan for Success

If you have not installed the main pond from which the water for the stream will be recycled, you can give full rein to your stream-dream. However, if you are adding a stream to an existing pond, you must

A tranquil stream gains interest from a stepped waterfall that breaches elevations.

determine the size stream that can be supported by the reservoir pond. The backyard stream contains a certain amount of water. When the recycling pump is turned on in the pond, water first fills the streambed before re-entering the pond. A specific amount of water is removed from the main pond when the stream is in operation.

Two disasters result if the reservoir pond is too small for the stream: the water level in the main pond drops a significant amount, endangering plants and animals and looking ugly as several inches of the pond walls appear; and the reservoir pond floods during periods of heavy rain or when the pump is turned off. The most beautiful design cannot make up for either miscalcula-

tion or noncalculation of the required size of the reservoir pond. Eamonn Hughes suggests that you estimate the necessary operating volume for the courseway by measuring the surface area of the streambed. Multiply length times width to determine the approximate square footage in the stream. Estimating that the water flow through the stream will be about three inches deep, Eamonn converts the three inches into a decimal percentage of one foot. By multiplying that figure by the square footage in the courseway, you determine the cubic measurement. Multiply the cubic measurement by 7.5 gallons in a cubic foot to find the approximate water volume required in the stream. So far, this is only

half the information you need to know. Next, determine how far the water will drop in the reservoir pond when the stream's operating volume is removed.

Since you want to know how many inches the pond water will drop, you need to know how much water is in one inch of your pond's entire surface. By multiplying length times width, you learn the pond's square footage. Multiply that figure by $\frac{1}{12}$ or .083 for one inch to determine the approximate volume of water in one inch depth of the pond. Again, multiply the cubic measurement that is given in percentage of feet by 7.5 gallons in a cubic foot to determine how many gallons are in the one-inch depth of water. When you divide the number of gallons in that one inch of water into the operating volume of your stream, you discover how much the water will drop during the stream's operation. (See chart in Chapter One.)

If your reservoir pond already exists, you may have to revise your stream plans to ensure the water does not drop significantly. If you have yet to install the main pond, you have the luxury of determining if you have enough space available to build both features to the desired and appropriate sizes. Once you have determined the sizes of the pond and the streambed, you can turn your attention to design and construction. As with any landscape amendment to the yard, the pond and stream should complement your existing design. An informal design can more closely replicate the waters found in nature. However, certain construction basics should be incorporated into your plans:

1. Water will flow from the top or most elevated point of the stream construction. This can be carved into the existing terrain or created by importing soil or using the soil from the pond excavation. Be sure to tamp imported soil well to alleviate natural settling and its resulting disruption of levels and design. Even better, import the soil and allow it to settle for as long as possible, even into the following season.

2. The longer the stream section, the deeper the top end of that section must be. To keep the stream shallow throughout, construct it in shorter sections. These sections do not need to be separated by great changes in elevation; very short "waterfall" breaks can define the sections. These breaks do not have to be flat rock falls either; a cobble "fall" or a weir drop of only a few inches creates both

Even a gentle slope offers a higher to lower flow route for water. Photo by H. Nash.

Changes in elevation can be accomplished with level stretches of the stream that tumble gently into the next level.

Photo by Eamonn Hughes.

interest and sound while subtly dividing the stream into the necessary shorter sections.

3. Water should attain a three-inch depth before tumbling into the next section. This three-inch depth should be determined so that it is below the surrounding ground level. Remember to incorporate the deeper level at the head of each section.

4. Plan the excavation to be deep enough to accommodate whatever size rocks or stones you will use to line the bed. Round cobbles require significantly more depth in excavation than decorative flat stones.

5. Plan the excavation to be deep enough to accommodate

To create bog planting areas along the stream, simply widen it and open a section of its length. Photo by Ron Everhart.

Many aquatic plants can be planted directly in the streambed. Photo by Ron Everhart.

whatever reinforcement needed beneath the courseway. If you plan to use large, heavy stones, provide either an appropriate concrete pad or several inches of compacted, crushed stone to prevent the stone from settling. Rocks that settle into the earth result in disruption of the construction and water loss.

6. Plan the excavation deeply enough to accommodate bog planting areas, if desired. These areas can be constructed as planting troughs with soil back-filled behind "retaining" stone walls that are constructed within the courseway. Decide whether to plant bog plants that tolerate moving water or calm water; this becomes part of your construction plan.

7. Use a level to ensure that both sides of the courseway are at the same level. While you may have a higher bank on one side of the courseway, remember that water remains level as it runs through the bed. Unless you want a pronounced difference between the height of the banks on each side, the water may appear lopsided.

8. Fully line the stream course. Simply cementing rocks together or cementing them into a bed of concrete or mortar does not ensure a leakproof bed. Concrete and mortar crumble and crack. By lining the course with a durable flexible liner, water will not be lost into the surrounding area. (Remember that this water is all coming from your reservoir pond; water loss in the stream ends up being water loss from the pond.) The liner should be brought far enough up the sides, at least four inches of the courseway, to capture any splash or high waters from rain, accumulating silt and debris, floating plants, or algae.

9. Plan for accessibility of services. Electricity is required to run the recirculating pump. Extension cords lying on the ground are dangerous. A licensed electrician is the best person to ensure safe electrical service. He/she will provide the proper ground fault circuit interrupter and safe installation of buried cables. When you begin construction of the feature, bury the hose from the pump to the top of the courseway in an accessible area. Do not place heavy stones on the hose that could complicate future service; bury the hose before building the final touches on the courseway.

10. Plan for variety. Interest is created by varying the width of the sections as well as their length. Since it is easier to construct with a minimum of folds in the liner, curves can be planned at the end of a section. Such planning works well with separate pieces of liner for each section, the upper level's liner overlapping the lower by several inches. Add more variety with small pools along the course that provide quiet areas for plants or bird beaches.

Mystery and Movement

As you plan the stream, remember the two "M's" of design: mystery and movement. Create mystery by hiding part of the

Mystery is created by simply hiding portions of the stream behind foreground plantings. Photo by Ron Everhart.

courseway. Hide the actual source of the water by covering the exit hose with rocks or by hiding it among plantings and rocks to create the illusion that the stream originates from much farther away. Provide a curve in the courseway immediately after the water entry to hide the source from the usual viewing point. If the course can be long enough, create bends in the stream so the viewer wonders what is just around the curve.

Movement provides sound and visual delight. It need not be confined to drops in levels of the course; it can be created by rocks within the streambed. A rock placed within the flow of water divides the water and provides impetus to the flow. Rocks need not be placed in the center of the bed; they may be off to the side, in effect creating narrower channels and faster water movement. While the excavation may be a uniform three feet across, the placement of stones and planting pockets provides variation in width and flow.

Stream Construction

Once you know the design and length of your stream, mark its outline on the ground with chalk, spray paint, cat litter, or rope. Dig the excavation itself as either a V or a U. Usually, the U excavation works better as it provides enough width in

A gently sloped stream is carved into the land, the liner laid in, and its primary lining rocks aligned along its length.

Photo by Eamonn Hughes.

A wide excavation leaves room for creating planting areas and varying rockwork. Note the carved and stepped areas for the changes in elevation.

Photo by Eamonn Hughes.

which to stack rocks and conceal the liner. A modified or slope-sided V will also work. However, be sure the excavation is not too narrow or too shallow to accommodate rocks that will conceal the liner and provide a natural appearance. The excavation should be deep enough to allow an inch or two of sand beneath the liner as well as whatever rocks are used in the finished design. Very large rocks can be included by digging out deeper holes in the courseway for them.

Dig and slope the excavation downward or dig it in level sections that proceed like stair steps to the entry into the reservoir pond. Check the side-to-side levels of the course as you excavate. In particularly uneven terrain, a tangent level and stakes to mark levels are helpful. However, keeping the sections short enough allows the use of a straightedge and carpenter's spirit level. (See Chapter Two.) It is likely that in providing the three-inch water depth before the exit into the next lower section, you will have a deeper section at the water's entry from the preceding or higher elevation. This is determined by using the carpenter's level as you measure and by maintaining the level from the head to the exit of the section while providing the three-inch water depth along the run.

The liner for the stream section may be a separate piece of membrane, but should overlap the lower-level pond reservoir liner.

Photo by Eamonn Hughes.

Since the stream is not excavated to the depth of the pond, most of the excavated soil will be topsoil and be of use for planting areas along the stream. If turf must be removed, take care to remove it in strips or squares to allow its use elsewhere.

Once the excavation is complete, provide reinforcement as necessary for heavy stones. If concrete pads will be used, be sure to reinforce them with heavy-grade wire mesh or rebar if your climate zone mandates a thickness of more than 4–6 inches. This concrete will be beneath the liner and will not

Once the liner is in place, set the spillways in mortar first.

Photo by Eamonn Hughes.

present leakage problems should it crack. Crushed stone or compacted limestone screening can be used for smaller rocks of 200 pounds or less. If spillways are created from one level to another, reinforce these areas to prevent settling and deterioration of your design.

Sweep the excavation clean of rocks, roots, and debris, and compact the soil base. Provide an inch or two of sand throughout the entire courseway to protect the liner. Moistened sand stays put better than dry sand. Fabric underlay may also be used. If the liner is installed in one piece, fit and fold it into the excavation and allow enough to extend over the sides

to confine all the water flow. Extend the stream liner over the pond liner by several inches. Any folds in the liner should be in the direction of the water flow to the reservoir pond. If a fabric underlay is used, cut it back above the pond's water level to prevent capillary action that wicks the water away from the pond into the surrounding soil. If the courseway is lined with separate pieces of liner, cover each section's length with one piece of liner that overlaps the next lower section by 3–6 inches. Again, be certain the fabric underlay does not extend beyond the spillway to wick away the water.

If you install concrete over the liner, do not cement rocks directly into the base. Brush the concrete with a wire brush to create a roughened surface. After the concrete has dried, apply additional concrete or mortar in which the rocks are set.

Consider mortaring the rocks to the liner. Loosely placed rocks invite water to flow beneath them rather than over them. Work from the lowest stream section back to the head or top. Build your stream walls first and then fit in any spillway rocks. Some professional builders use a spray poly foam that is available from hardware stores to affix rocks to the liner. The foam hardens quickly and seems to bond better with the

Working from the bottom up, mortar in the side stones and fill in the framework of the streambed. Photo by Eamonn Hughes.

liner material than concrete or mortar.

For short expanses, the cost of poly foam is comparable to mortar. However, one spray can will cover only 2–3 square feet in affixing rocks to the streambed. Very expansive in volume, it must be used cautiously as it billows out from between the rocks and later surprises you with more bubbles of yellow material oozed from between them. Camouflage these bubbles by tossing sand on them while the medium is still soft and pushing them back in with a stick. Do not use poly foam with your bare hands as it is difficult to remove from them.

Any bubbles that harden between rocks can be twisted off. While the use of this product seems an easy alternative to mortar, a non-obtrusive and natural appearance is difficult to obtain. The product's best use may be as an out-of-sight, waterproof backfilling.

Vary the sizes of rocks in the bed. Place stratified rocks in the same direction for the most natural appearance. Set broken rocks to appear as though they

Pebbles set in mortar create a naturally appearing streambed. Note the use of larger pebbles and cobbles near the stream's edge. Photo by Eamonn Hughes.

extend deeper into the streambed. Rocks placed within the streambed create interest in the water flow and produce increased velocity as the water emerges from them. Line the informal, natural stream with round cobbles or river stones, and line a formal stream with decorative pebbles or bricks.

Create planting troughs so that water seeps into the soil held

Adding a dye to it makes the mortar between the stones less obvious.

Photo by Greg Maxwell.

within them to grow bog plantings. Add staggered timber accents by embedding them in a pad of concrete or mortar. Either seal any concrete or mortar or scrub it well with a 5:1 muriatic acid and water solution to prevent lime from leaching into the water and endangering fish. If you cannot properly seal the mortar, rinse it well with vinegar and run the water through the courseway long enough to leach out dangerous levels of lime before fish are

Decorative wood edging that is set in mortar within the streambed creates a bog-plant area at the stream's edge.

Photo by Greg Maxwell.

added or returned to the pond below. (Use a pH test kit to monitor the lime level. A reading above 8 indicates the probability of lime leaching into the water.)

When you reach the top of the streambed, create a grotto or concealed entry for the hose and bury it alongside the stream. Another option is to create a smaller header pool that

leads into the courseway. This header pond may also be a natural filter pond in which bog plants help purify the system's water.

The Formed Stream

Wooden forms are set approximately four inches in from the edge of the stream's excavation.

Photo by Greg Maxwell.

Depending on climate recommendations and the thickness of the concrete form, heavy wire mesh or chicken wire may reinforce the concrete form.

Photo by Greg Maxwell.

Wooden strips can be used for both sides of the stream's forms.

Photo by Greg Maxwell.

Lay in the liner and begin covering it with rocks.

Photo by Greg Maxwell.

Remove the forms once the concrete has set.

Photo by Greg Maxwell.

Finishing Touches

With the water hose buried accessibly, add the final touches to the stream course. Avoid lining up a row of rocks along the perimeter. Extend some out into the surrounding terrain; embed them partially in the soil to appear natural. Edging plants such as daylilies with fountain foliage provide variety and interest to the stream edge. Grace shady areas with ferns and other lush shade-loving plants. Moisture-loving plants such as water forget-me-not (*Myosotis palustris),* water irises, and *primula* work well, too. Consider other low-maintenance treatments along the stream that are in keeping with the treatment around the reservoir pond. Rock gardens, ornamental grasses, decorative stone, mulch, specimen plantings, and other low-maintenance plantings maximize the time spent enjoying the creation.

The stream presents a creative way to tie the elements of your landscape together, whether those elements be shade to sun or pond to pond. With careful planning, a natural stream feature enhances the magic and tranquility of your private backyard haven.

Once the walls of the stream are mortared, you can begin designing the bed.

Photo by Eamonn Hughes.

Juncus patens *is planted in the edge of the streambed. To prevent plants from eventually damming the water, thin them as needed.*

Photo by Eamonn Hughes.

An uneven front edge to the spillway rock produces a split water flow.

Photo by Eamonn Hughes.

Stream Design Tips

Smaller pebbles on a flat stream course will produce a tranquil flow. Photo by Eamonn Hughes.

Finishing up the edge of the streambed, pebbles line a shallow beach that will invite birds and wildlife. Photo by Eamonn Hughes.

With water running through the streambed, the pebbles produce a gentle ripple. Use a large volume of water along a streambed of river rocks of ⅜" to 3" in size. Allow for 3–6" of water in the stream bed.

Photo by Eamonn Hughes.

Setting river rocks in the streambed produces riffles in the shallow stream. If you want more movement on the water's surface, add more river rock until the surface is broken.

Photo by Eamonn Hughes.

Water flows over flat weir rocks at elevation changes in the courseway.

Photo by Eamonn Hughes.

The End of the Stream

One way to ease the flow of a stream entering the reservoir pond is to quiet its waters with a smaller pond before its final re-entry. Photo by Eamonn Hughes.

A well-spaced two-tiered waterfall allows the stream's waters to announce their arrival.

Photo by Eamonn Hughes.

The Hidden Reservoir Stream

With the irrigation cover-lid removed, you can see the pipe that runs from the pump in the reservoir tank to the waterfall/stream.

Photo by Eamonn Hughes.

A 100-foot-long stream is serviced by a 1000-gallon reservoir.

Photo by Eamonn Hughes.

Although constructed in a small area, the curved stream appears longer as it exits into a narrow channel of the pond transversed by a miniature railway trestle. Photo by H. Nash..

Stream Inspirations

A narrow rivulet tumbles through the shady understory of a woodland stream.

Photo by Eamonn Hughes.

The peace and harmony inherent in Japanese garden design is typified by the quiet stream waters. Photo by H. Nash.

PUMP SELECTION & INSTALLATION

Tranquility is the key to a slowly moving stream that winds through the property.

Part of planning a moving water feature is deciding what type and size pump will move the waters. Although the submersible pump is most commonly used, you may opt for an external, or centrifugal, pump.

Types of Pumps

The submersible pump is placed directly in the pond, usually propped at a small distance from the bottom to prevent silt and debris from clogging the intake. Water is pumped directly from the pond to the waterfall or stream. Submersible pumps used for fountain assemblies must be set upon a plinth or block so the attached fountain head emerges from the water. Advantages to submersible pumps are their lack of noise and that they do not need dry housing outside the pond, as well as that they can also be used to drain the pond.

Small pumps are affixed easily to fountain heads. Note the valve attachment that can control other fixtures to the same water source.

Photo by Oliver Jackson.

The major disadvantage of a submersible pump is its relative inaccessibility. Filter attachments and screens hampered by pond debris require cleaning, at least occasionally. In early spring and in late summer to autumn, this chore may be required every week. Some pondkeepers ingeniously rig ways to remove the pump without having to wade into or reach down into the pond. Care must be taken to provide a fine-meshed screen over the pump's inlet to prevent the loss of small fish or tadpoles.

Another disadvantage (though

rare) is that the pump seal can rupture, allowing the oil coolant to escape. Recent improvements in manufacturing and the use of double seals make this unlikely with newer pumps. Also, a new line of magnetic-drive submersible pumps completely avoids the use of oil as a motor coolant.

The external, or centrifugal, pump offers accessibility for routine maintenance or repairs. Likewise, if the pump fails, there is no danger of water contamination. These pumps need to be housed somewhere near the pond or water feature. Finding a creative and attractive means to do this can be a problem. Centrifugal pumps are notorious for losing their priming water, the water that must fill the impeller housing before the pump will operate. Often this requires a manual filling of the housing.

Filter units can also be added to the pump to filter debris and provide biological filtration to fish-inhabited waters.

Photo by Oliver Jackson.

A submersible sump-type pump draws water in from beneath and cycles it through the outlet on the arm extrusion.

Photo by Eamonn Hughes.

Many water gardeners who require larger pumps than the smaller ones commonly sold for water gardens have discovered they need not turn to the external pumping system. Industrial-size sump pumps offer the greater pumping capacities required for large waterfall and stream systems. Still generally available in blue rather than the more easily hidden black like water garden submersibles, they can be easily camouflaged within the reservoir pond by a shelf or platform.

With the increase in the cost of electricity to run pumps, manufacturers have developed high-efficiency pumps. These pumps often require less than half the power to operate than traditional pumps. At this time, their initial cost is significantly more than standard pumps. Before you decide on a pump, check with dealers to compare initial and operating costs, and apprise yourself of any new developments.

Sizes of Pump

Pump size is generally calculated by the gallons per hour (GPH) output at one foot of lift or height. Larger pumps are rated by horsepower (hp). Manufacturers offer charts that break down the power of each size pump according to incremental heights of one foot. While some pumps are labeled by the GPH size, other lines of pump are given letter or number designations that require reference to the chart.

To determine the size pump required for your waterfall project, estimate the vertical height from the top of your pump to the top of the waterfall. Note that some builders estimate this distance from the top of the pond water. If the pump is set in two feet of water, there is a difference of two feet in lift. For the larger project, the difference in water flow is minimal. In a smaller project, however, such as a one-foot-high waterfall for a two-foot-deep pond, the difference in flow rate is 120 gallons per hour versus only 70 gallons per hour. Since you can always decrease the flow through valving but cannot increase it, using the computation from the top of the pump may be best. In addition to the maximum height, for every ten feet of piping or hosing that the water must be moved, another foot in height must be added to the lift capacity required of the pump. This allows for the loss in volume from resistance within the pipe.

For a reasonable flow of water, a general rule of thumb is to figure your waterfall/stream requirement as 150 gallons per hour per inch width of spillway or channel. For example, if your stream or waterfall spillway will be ten inches wide, you will need a pump to produce a flow of 1500 gallons per hour. The heights of waterfalls are easily determined. The height of a stream courseway that meanders over some length may require the use of a tangent to learn the actual highest elevation. Hopefully, you noted such measurements on the graph drawing made in your initial planning. If the hose connecting from the pump to the head of the feature is 30 feet long, you will have to consider an additional 3 feet (one foot of lift per 10 feet of hose) to be added to the lift of the feature. Once you know the total lift in feet, you can refer to the pump charts. Follow the column down that corresponds to your height until you find the closest figure to the gallons per hour you need. Should your requirement fall between two pump sizes, select the larger. If the total lift is 10 feet and you need 1500 gallons per hour, you see from the charts that a Little Giant 6 series pump produces slightly more than the flow you need. By using a valve, you can adjust the pump's flow to what you want.

Pump Size Chart for Pumps by Lifts in Feet

Lifts	1'	3'	5'	10'	15'	20'
			Gallons Per Hour			
	120	70				
	170	140	100			
	205	168	120			
	300	255	205	70		
	325	300	270	130		
	500	435	337	210	65	
	600	580	517	414	230	90
	710	690	670	580	380	150
	810	790	745	613	415	173
	1200	1170	1100	1000	840	520
⅙hp				900	690	480
0.3hp				2750	1750	750
0.4hp				3250	2500	1550

Little Giant Pump Size Chart

Pump model	5'	10'	15'
6 series	2750	1759	750
6E series	3000	2500	1600
8 series	250	2500	1550
10 series	4200	3800	2700
12 series	5000	4000	3000

Plumbing

The two main choices of pipework to carry water from your pond to the waterfall are rigid pipe or flexible tubing. Rigid PVC pipe is the least expensive, but it requires glued elbows and adapters to join everything together. Always use the *white* form of PVC as water run through it is potable and safe for fish. Since PVC is a plastic, multiple-component silicones, epoxies, and superglues will attack and degrade it. Use *single component silicone* for gluing any joints and adapters. Most single-component silicones

Flexible tubing will be hooked up to the pump's outlet for recycling water through a waterfall or stream. Photo by Eamonn Hughes.

Bulkhead fittings and hose barbs make adjustments as needed to control the flow of water desired. Photo by Bob Romar, courtesy of Maryland Aquatic Nurseries.

contain acetic acid that you can smell. *Acetic acid is corrosive to brass, copper, and bronze.* If the joints you must glue will come into contact with any of these metals, use *neutral cure silicone,* which does not emit the corrosive acid. More expensive and requiring a longer cure period, this form of single-component silicone is safe to use. *As a sealant, silicone needs at least 24 hours' exposure to air and humidity to cure.* As an adhesive, the bonding cure may require a week's exposure to air and humidity. A ⅛- to ¼-inch-diameter bead of the product achieves maximum strength. Thicker layers require more drying time and are weaker. Should any portion of the white PVC piping be exposed to sunlight, perhaps where the pipe leaves the ground to re-enter the water feature system, paint the pipe black. This prevents the plastic from deteriorating

and turning brittle and cracking.

Class 200 (thin wall) PVC is available in diameters of ½", ¾", and 1". For larger diameters, use Schedule 40 (thick wall) PVC. Usually the size of the outlet port on the pump is appropriate to its flow. Many professionals and pondkeepers feel that adapting the port to the next larger diameter produces a more satisfactory flow, particu-

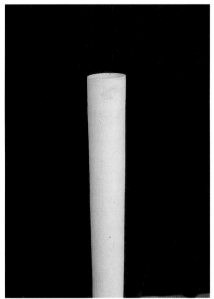

White, potable PVC piping provides rigid water return when desired. Photo by Eamonn Hughes.

larly with waterfalls. Likewise, if the tubing is of any significant length, adapting to the next larger diameter may be warranted. Eamonn Hughes recommends adapting the size up by one-half to one inch to reduce friction loss if the delivery hose is longer than 50 feet. A ball valve added near the pump allows control by as much as 50 percent of the flow. Check the operating instructions of the pump before purchase to be certain your desired reduction is acceptable. If you elect to close down the valve to any degree, watch for further restriction of flow that indicates trapped debris in the line; relieve the blockage and avoid stressing the pump by opening and closing the valve.

Flexible Piping

The flexible tubing commonly available in the smaller diameters used for fountains and piped statuary is often clear plastic. Especially if the tubing is exposed to sunlight, algae quickly build up inside the tube to create resistance and decreased flow. Trying to clean a length of narrow tubing is awkward if not impossible. Rather than frequent replacement of the tubing, use black plastic tubing that blocks out light and discourages the algae growth.

A common means of water delivery in the ½-inch to 1-inch range is garden hoses. A very flexible, reinforced, all-weather hose will usually do the job. Avoid using unsuitable hose that may split open in freezing climates.

Eamonn has been using a flexible, reinforced spa hose for a number of years and has found it so easy to install that the extra cost has been worth it to him. If you use a flexible hose, he recommends that it be reinforced to avoid hose wall collapse and restricted flow. Eamonn notes an advantage of maximum flow from less in-line resistance than through rigid pipes with elbow attachments.

If you decide to have a number of water movements in your water garden, use one pump to feed them all by gluing tees into the delivery line with ball valves on each tee. Adjust the various flows by closing each tee to a different degree.

Plumbing a Spouting Ornament

Plastic tubing is fitted over the water outlet on the pump.
Photo by Eamonn Hughes.

The other end of the plastic tubing is threaded into the ornament or statue to emit water as desired. Photo by Eamonn Hughes.

Recommended Tubing Diameter for Pumps to Waterfalls

½ inch diameter	for flows up to	120 GPH
¾ inch diameter	for flows up to	350 GPH
1 inch diameter	for flows up to	1000 GPH
1¼ inch diameter	for flows up to	1500 GPH
1½ inch diameter	for flows up to	3000 GPH

Pump Maintenance

How much attention is required by the pump depends on how clean the waters are that it circulates. Water containing suspended particles—be they soil, organic matter, or algae—deposits this material on the intake port. Many pumps come equipped with a mesh screen covering the intake.

Submersible bottom-intake pumps with only a grate over the intake and submerged open-port pumps should be supplied with appropriate screen protection. Particulate matter unnecessarily stresses and shortens the life of the pump. The larger this screen area, the less frequently it needs cleaning.

Whether you wrap your pump in a fine fiberglass screen or affix a filter media box to the intake side of the pump, at some point it requires cleaning. If you do not monitor the status of the intake filter, watch for reduced water flow through your feature. In extreme cases, the pump's filter becomes so filthy that it produces fish-toxic methane and hydrogen sulfide gases by anaerobic bacterial activity. The gases may cause the filter box to rise in the water, disconnect from the pump, and float on the water's surface.

Early spring and early autumn are generally the periods of highest organic loading in the pond. Check the pump's filter screen often, at least weekly, during this time. Shut off the pump and remove it and its filter attachments from the water to hose them clean with a strong jet of water. Replace filter media as needed.

With external pumps, check the filter media and screening provisions to clean as necessary. Sand filter (swimming-pool type) units require backwashing as needed. With heavy bioloads, backwash at least once weekly to avoid toxic anaerobic activity within the media and to prevent "channeling"—the development of water flowing out around the media rather than down through it—producing a reduced effectiveness and flow.

Many pondkeepers run the submerged pump throughout the winter season. In all but the coldest of climates, the moving water escapes total freezing. However, the pump should be moved into the top third of the reservoir pond's waters to avoid circulating colder air-cooled and surface waters into the lower, warmer waters where fish "hibernate."

If the submerged pump serves a fountain assembly, remove the pump and fountain to disconnect them and clean. Store the fountain assembly for the winter. Set up the pump at the water's surface, where the outflow port allows recirculated waters to bubble and maintain an ice-free area, or store the pump appropriately for the season.

In very shallow reservoir waters that serve fountain assemblies or very small ponds, the pump should be removed for the freezing winter period. Clean the pump and store it in a non-freezing area. Store the pump containing oil coolant in a bucket of water to prevent the seals from drying, cracking, and producing oil leaks. Magnetic-drive pumps may be stored dry.

Clean and disconnect the centrifugal, external pump in freezing areas. Leave all bottom valves open so all water drains from the unit.

FOUNTAINS & MOVING WATER FEATURES

Water flowing from the statue's ewer only enhances the beauty of this classic statue.

Froth, foam, geysers, sparkling droplets, shimmering sprays, and glistening ribbons—fountains offer art in motion. Inviting this magical form of moving water into your garden can be as simple as a fountain head kit or a piped statue.

From a Simple Kit

Inexpensive fountain head kits offer a variety of moving waters: a single surging jet, tiered or umbrella-shaped droplets, a gleaming inverted bowl, a ring of slender, arching streams, or an oscillating dance of entwining waters. The least expensive of these kits are black plastic units that attach to pump outlets. Often the kits come equipped with several interchangeable, snap-on heads to vary the spray patterns. The fountain is set up with the head attached to the outlet port of a submerged pump and the fountain head is outside

The simplest kit for a small pond consists of a small submersible pump with the outlet through a fountain head. This kit offers a filtration attachment to aid in preventing blockages in the head. Photo courtesy of Rena Corporation.

Brass fixtures will not oxidize in water. This kit is shown with a submerged light that creates nighttime magic.

Photo by Oliver Jackson.

the water. The kits may be sold with or without a pump. Installation requires a safe electrical outlet served through a ground fault circuit interrupter and a stable, level position for the pump and its attached fountain head. Dave Artz, a Texas landscape designer, suggests using an upside-down flower

pot to stabilize the fountain; simply thread the hose through the hole in the bottom of the pot. Use a carpenter's spirit level to ascertain the base's level. A ball valve in the line from the pump provides handy control of the water flow. Provide camouflage for the wiring.

With the water jets aimed to the center, the ringed fountain head can be used in a very small pond. Photo by Oliver Jackson.

A rotating fountain head allows the water's pattern to constantly change. Photo by Gordon T. Ledbetter.

A tiered fountain pattern captures the early morning sunlight. Photo by Gordon T. Ledbetter.

Large floating fountains capture sunlight in rare rainbows as they aerate the lake's waters. Photo courtesy of Otterbine Corporation.

A simple fountain spray brings life to a small preformed pond.

Photo by Clifford Tallman.

Known as a foaming fountain head, this fountain lends sound, sight, and beneficial aeration to the small koi pond. Photo by Carol Christensen.

*A combined fountain head pro-
duces both a foaming and a jet
spray of water.* Photo by Charles Henne.

*The bell fountain flow captivates
young Grace Chen at the
Children's Discovery Garden in
Longwood Gardens,
Pennsylvania.* Photo by H. Nash.

Even a small fountain spray provides a lively patter to the small pond.

Photo by Ron Everhart.

Fountain heads are designed to produce a variety of sprays.

Photo by Charles Henne.

A unique variation on the floating fountain, a clamp on the water intake hose controls the spread of the lily's spray.

Photo by H. Nash.

A single jet rises powerfully from the pond's waters to provide aesthetic enjoyment even from a distance. Photo by Carol Christensen.

Rena Small Fountain Pump Chart

Height:	0'	1'	2'	3'	4'	5'	6'	Max. Ht.	Diam. (Bell)
Model				Gallons Per Hour					
20 Series	53	45	10					2'4"	8"
40 Series	160	128	96	64	32			5'	16"
40T Series	264	226	188	150	112	74	37	7'	
60 Series	525	486	432	378	324	279	216	10'	24"

The above-listed pumps are magnetically driven centrifugal pumps for use in tub gardens, fountains, statuary, and small to medium-size water gardens.

Rena Pumps

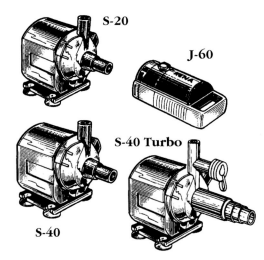

S-20

J-60

S-40 Turbo

S-40

Rena Pumps are now part of Aquarium Pharmaceuticals.

Rena Fountain Spray Patterns

Two small jets with extensions for thin, single spray

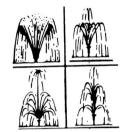

Flower spray with four inter-changeable diffusers

Rotating triple jet

Rotating and swiveling jet

Swiveling arc jet

Flower spray

Little Giant Small Pump Chart for Fountains and Small Ponds

Height:	1'	3'	5'	10'	15'	Maximum Height
Model			Gallons Per Hour			
PES-A	63					
PE-A	80	45				4.5'
P-AAA-WG	120	70				4.6'
PE-1-WG	170	140	100			7'
PE-2F-WG	300	270	240	130		12.2'
NK-2UL-WG	325	300	270	130		10'
PE-2.5F-WG	475	440	395	205		13.4'

For Larger Fountains

	1'	3'	5'	10'	15'	Maximum Height
5-MSP-WG	1200	1170	1110	1000	840	17.3'
6-CIM-R			2750	1750	750	18'
6E-CIM			3000	2500	1600	18'
8-CIM			3250	2500	1550	23'
10-CIM			4200		2700	23'

Mushroom Spray

For a showy but gentle splash, use with the PE-1 for a 17" diameter spray. The PE-2.5 pump gives a 36" diameter spray, and the PE-2F gives a 28" spray. The NK-2 produces a 2' spray.

Little Giant Pumps

PE-A

PE-A. 80 GPH. $^{1}/_{8}$" MNPT outlet with $^{3}/_{8}$" barb for tubing.

PE-1-WG

PE-1-WG. 170 GPH. $^{1}/_{4}$" MNPT outlet.

NK-2UL-WG

NK-2UL. 325 GPH. $^{1}/_{4}$" MNPT with 90-degree elbow accessory.

PE2.5F-WG

PE2.5F. 475 GPH. $^{3}/_{8}$" MNPT outlet accepts $^{5}/_{8}$" diameter tubing.

Oase Pump Chart

Height	1'	3'	5'	9'	Pumps to	Nozzle Size
Model		Gallons Per Hour				
Aquarius 4		160				
Aquarius 6		245				
Aquarius 8	340	280	200	90	7'	
Nautilus 10	660	630	550	240	10.8'	½"
Nautilus 30	1200	1100	950	470	13.1'	1"
Nautilus 45	1600	1330	1110	670	15'	1"

Oase is a German company that has been manufacturing pumps for nearly 50 years. Its products are oil-free and may offer ceramic bearings along with stainless-steel housings that do not corrode in water.

Oase Pumps

Aquarius series   *Nautilus series*

Oase Fountain Head Sprays

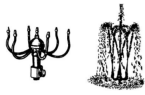

¹/₂" Pirouette Fountain Head

1" Bell/Cascade Fountain Head

1" Blossom Fountain Head

1" Frothy Fountain Head

Nozzle and Pump
Recommendations from Oase

½" Pirouette Fountain Head (maximum spray dimensions are 42" height x 16" diameter): Aquarius 8

1" Bell/Cascade Fountain Head (maximum spray dimensions are 12" height x 10" diameter): Nautilus 10

1" Bell/Cascade Fountain Head (maximum spray dimensions are 24" height x 32" diameter): Nautilus 30

1" Bell/Cascade Fountain Head (maximum spray dimensions are 36" height x 60" diameter): Nautilus 45

1" Blossom Fountain Head (maximum spray dimensions are 24" height x 18" diameter): Nautilus 10

1" Blossom Fountain Head (maximum spray dimensions are 60" height x 30" diameter): Nautilus 30

1" Blossom Fountain Head (maximum spray dimensions are 72" height x 60" diameter): Nautilus 45

1" Frothy Fountain Head (maximum spray dimensions are 15" height x 10" diameter): Nautilus 10

1" Frothy Fountain Head (maximum spray dimensions are 26" height x 10" diameter): Nautilus 30

1" Frothy Fountain Head (maximum spray dimensions are 31" height x 21" diameter): Nautilus 45

Oase Fountain Accessories

Fountain Head Assortment: The kits come with a telescopic stem and a diverter valve. The telescopic lens extends from 8" up to 14". The flow regulator valve adjusts the flow directly to the fountain head or to statuary using ⅜"-diameter tubing. These may be used with pumps up to 340 gallons per hour at a one-foot lift.

½" Flow Regulator: This adjusts the flow to the fountain head or to a diverter outlet. Attach ½"-diameter tubing to a diverter outlet to operate a waterfall or statuary. This is also available in a 1" size and attaches to ¾"-diameter tubing.

Telescopic Extension (1" diameter): Use this with larger pumps in the 1200–1600 gallons per hour at a one-foot lift range. This adjusts the fountain head height from 10" to 20".

Underwater Lights: These are available in wattages from 36 to 120. Wired into GFI-protected circuitry, they must be used with low-voltage outdoor transformers that can accommodate up to four plugs. The transformers may offer automatic timers, too.

Color Wheel: A four-section (red, green, orange, and white) wheel rotates with the thrust of the pump at an adjustable speed. Working with submerged lighting, the wheel casts colored light on the flowing fountain.

Telescopic Extension

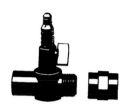

2-Way Valve. The diverter outlet connects to flexible tubing. The valve outlet fits ½" MNPT fountain nozzle stems. The valve inlet is ½" MNPT with ½" FNPT adapter; it fits a ½" MNPT pump outlet.

Known as the "Gusher" in the Little Giant product line, this fountain head produces a frothy head only 3 inches high with a 170 GPH pump. A 14-inch-high column is produced with a 325 GPH pump, and a 24-inch-high column is produced with a 475 GPH pump.

4-Pack Fountain Head Assortment

Flow Regulator

Larger Fountains

The primary difference between the installation of small and large fountains is the support base the unit sits on. If the larger fountain is only a fountain head attached to a pump, the procedure remains the same. Enclosed within heavy stonework, the fountain should be set level and firmly upon a solid plinth or platform. Often these require additional support both below and over the pond liner. A substantial concrete slab, reinforced if necessary, is installed before laying the liner in the reservoir pond. Another layer of liner or padding is used on top of the liner to protect it from punctures. If you use concrete blocks to build the fountain support, either paint them with black sealing paint or rinse them with vinegar or put them through numerous washings to prevent lime from leaching into waters inhabited by fish.

Plumbed Statuary

Garden statuary adds an artistic dimension to the garden. Plumbed statuary and flowing water enhance that aspect. Small ornaments such as cherubs, frogs, or turtles may be set poolside to emit a single stream of water. These features may be plumbed directly to

Large statuary may be plumbed in more than one place for added interest.

Photo by Richard Sacher, courtesy of American Aquatic Gardens.

their own small pump (see preceding charts) or they may be diverted from a larger pump that services a waterfall or stream. Use black tubing for their water routing to avoid algae buildup in the tubing that will affect the flow.

Any small object that allows a plastic tube inside to an egress can be used as a plumbed water feature-urns or hand-pumps, for example. The only requirement is that an inconspicuous point of water tube entry be provided. Pottery used as a water feature should be sealed if the water will be contained in it before flowing out.

A delightful variety of plumbed statuary offers selections suitable to any garden design. If the statuary will be set up within a pond, provide a

Although a strong flow of water is produced, its force is dissipated enough by the time it reaches the pond's surface not to disturb nearby water lilies.

Photo by Anita Nelson.

solid and level support so the feature cannot topple over. If the statue and its support weigh more than 200 pounds, provide a concrete support pad beneath the pond liner and an appropriate protective layer over the liner.

If you would feature the statue apart from a pond setting, provide a hidden reservoir of water from which to circulate. This can be as simple as a buried heavy-duty plastic barrel. Determine how many gallons per hour the pump requires to operate the feature and provide that amount within the reservoir. Conceal the reservoir beneath ground cover, cobbles, or turf. Heavy statuary requires a solid support, such as a reinforced concrete base, to ensure its stability.

Determine the pump required by the height of the statue and reference to a manufacturer's pump chart.

Two cherubs cavort with the water in this pond.

Photo by Richard Sacher, courtesy of American Aquatic Gardens.

A Japanese-styled pouring fountain graces a small water feature. Photo by H. Nash.

Gently cascading waters trickle from the statue's shells.

Photo by Ron Everhart.

"Le Bâtre Fountain Clock" is interpreted with modern sculpture.

Designed, copyrighted, and photographed by Gordon T. Ledbetter.

A plumbed turtle statue spouts a steady stream of water from poolside. Photo by Ron Everhart.

A plumbed frog statue introduces the sound of water.

Photo by Ron Everhart.

Plumbed statuary is available in cast concrete in many designs.

Photo by Oliver Jackson.

The original "Le Bâtre Fountain Clock" was designed by Gordon T. Ledbetter, the internationally known Irish designer.

Photo by Gordon T. Ledbetter.

A trio of cherubs spray water into the pond.

Photo by Ron Everhart.

A foaming fountain head set within a Japanese lantern recycles water.

Photo by H. Nash, courtesy of Reimer Waterscapes®.

Wall Fountains

Traditionally, wall fountains are classically designed, such as in the form of spouting gargoyles. However, any flat-sided sculpture can be used as a wall fountain if it is provided with a hole from which the water may spout. Nor is a sculpture necessary; the fountain may flow from a spigot in a stucco, stone, or brick wall. The water can spew forth or trickle down the face. All that is required is a reservoir of water and a recirculating pump. Use either a basin of water or a concealed reservoir for the water. Since no fish are involved, the water can be treated with chemical algaecides to maintain clarity. Particularly if the feature is in sunlight, scrub the feature to prevent unsightly algae stains.

Southwestern architectural design interprets the spouting wall fountain.

Photo by Charles Henne.

The wall fountain need not be elaborate; this one is elegant in its simplicity. Photo by Charles Henne.

Terra-cotta wall fountains are affixed to a fence to return water to the pond below.

Photo by Scott Bates.

A courtyard entryway features a spraying and overflowing fountain and a wall fountain. Designed and photographed by Gordon T. Ledbetter.

Wall fountains are available in a variety of classic designs.

Photo courtesy of Design Toscano.

A simple fountain emerges from a pipe in the wall.

Photo by H. Nash.

Other Plumbed
Water Features

Peter Davidson adapts the classic bamboo spout shi-shi odoshi into a tabletop water feature.

Photo by Peter Davidson, Zen Water Gardens.

An antique interpretation of the hand pump is plumbed to recycle water through a small basin. Photo by Ron Everhart.

By routing the tubing from the submerged pump below, water constantly flows from the old-fashioned hand pump.

Photo by H. Nash.

An overflowing ladle returns water to this pond.

Photo by Ron Everhart.

Miniature waterwheels are available in kits, as are full-size versions such as this one.

Photo by H. Nash.

Millstones and Spilling Waters

The millstone is a slightly concave stone circle with a plumbed tunnel in the center that water flows through. The water gathers within the slight depression and then spills over the stone's edge. Traditional millstones are surrounded by cobbles or pebbles that allow the overflowing waters to flow through them into a reservoir below. A strong grate covers the reservoir to hold the cobbles above. Millstones provide a soft gurgle of water in a childproof setting. They can be adapted, however, to pond situations. Set the millstone above the water level to create a gentle cascade all around, or set it within or at the water level. The millstone is particularly attractive to birds and offers a unique birdbath and drinking basin. Usually the millstone involves a foaming water exit that is only a few inches high. Smaller volumes are used. However, a foot-high frothy column is achieved with a 660-gallon-per-hour pump.

Fountain Maintenance

Unless the fountain operates from sterile waters kept chemically clean, provide a prefilter unit to maintain the purity of

Child-safe cobbled reservoir fountains feature bubbling or foaming waters that rise from the rocks. Here, glass balls glisten with the flowing water. Photo by H. Nash, courtesy of Reimer Waterscapes®.

Another version of the millstone set within a pond allows the water to flow directly from the stone into the surrounding water.
Photo by H. Nash, courtesy of Reimer Waterscapes®.

water circulating through the pump and fountain accessory. Monitor the filter unit and hose it clean as necessary. Fountains with small holes may still clog. When you notice this happening, shut off the fountain and use cotton swabs or a toothpick or any other device with a fine point to clear the holes. Scrub the outlets with a bristle brush to prevent algae stains. If fish are kept in the waters, use only salt as a cleaning abrasive.

Fountain features kept in freezing climate areas are shut down and stored for the winter. (See Chapter 5.)

European Inspirations

The gardens of the Villa d'Este display many ways water can move. Photo by Gordon T. Ledbetter.

In St. Paul de Vence, France, a drinking fountain and animal water trough offer respite.

Photo by Eamonn Hughes.

An intricately crafted fountain nozzle ejects water in the courtyard fountain in Temple sur Lot, France. Photo by Eamonn Hughes.

A modern concrete-and-tile fountain bowl interprets flowing waters in Temple sur Lot, France. Photo by Eamonn Hughes.

Inspirations from Public Fountains

The "Las Colinas" fountains in Dallas, Texas, display sculpted animals with frothy waters emerging at their feet.

Photo by Anita Nelson.

From the Arizona Centre, Scottsdale, comes a pinwheel design of foaming fountains in a tiled depression.

Photo by Charles Henne.

Use multiples of simple fountain jets to create artful water designs. Photo by Charles Henne.

From Leu Gardens in Florida, we see the stunning effect of a row of equally calibrated foaming fountains. Photo by Marsha Alley.

Sculpted basins combine with a foaming center display for artistic waters. Photo by Charles Henne.

Separate fountain heads create design at the water's surface.
Photo by Charles Henne.

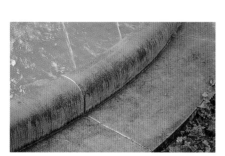

Individual streams of water can be fit within the perimeter of a formal display. Photo by H. Nash.

The Phoenician Resort, Scottsdale, offers a breathtaking display of graduated jets of water to form a shimmering pyramid.
Photo by Charles Henne.

APPENDIX

Plants for the Stream Garden

The following plants are suitable for planting right in the flowing water of the side of a stream. Select a variety of plants according to their texture, color, growth habit, flowering time, hardiness for your area, and general appeal.

Butomus umbellatus

Flowering rush

Height: 3'

Zone: 6

Blooms: Spring-Summer

Aspect: Sun

Photo by Ron Everhart.

Calla palustris

Bog arum

Height: 1'

Zone: 5

Blooms: Spring-Summer

Aspect: Shade

Photo by Eamonn Hughes.

Caltha palustris

Yellow marsh marigold

Height: 1'

Zone: 5

Blooms: Spring-Summer

Aspect: Shade

Photo by Eamonn Hughes.

Caltha palustris 'Flora plena'
Double yellow marsh marigold
Height: 18"
Zone: 5
Blooms: Spring-Summer
Aspect: Shade

Photo by Eamonn Hughes.

Cyperus alternifolius
Umbrella palm
Height: 3'
Zone: 8
Blooms: Summer
Aspect: Sun

Photo by Ron Everhart.

Eleocharis palustris

Common spike rush

Height: 1'

Zone: 3

Blooms: Spring

Aspect: Sun

Photo by Eamonn Hughes.

Houttuynia cordata

Houttuynia

Height: 18"

Zone: 5

Blooms: Summer

Aspect: Part shade

Photo by Eamonn Hughes.

Houttuynia cordata 'Variegata'

Chameleon plant

Height: 18"

Zone: 5

Blooms: Summer

Aspect: Part shade

Photo by Eamonn Hughes.

Iris pseudacorus

Yellow flag iris

Height: 3'

Zone: 5

Blooms: Spring

Aspect: Sun

Photo by Eamonn Hughes.

Iris versicolor

Blue flag iris

Height: 18"

Zone: 6

Aspect: Part shade

Photo by Ron Everhart.

Mimulus guttatus

Yellow monkey flower

Height: 1'

Zone: 4

Blooms: Summer

Aspect: Sun

Photo by Eamonn Hughes.

Peltandra virginica

Spoonflower

Height: 2'

Zone: 5

Blooms: Summer

Aspect: Part shade

Photo by Eamonn Hughes.

Pontederia cordata

Purple pickerel weed

Height: 20"

Zone: 3

Blooms: Summer-Fall

Aspect: Sun

Photo by Eamonn Hughes.

Pontederia cordata 'Alba'

White pickerel weed

Height: 2'

Zone: 3

Blooms: Summer-Fall

Aspect: Sun

Photo by Eamonn Hughes.

Sagittaria latifolia

Arrowhead

Height: 2'

Zone: 3

Blooms: Summer

Aspect: Sun

Photo by Eamonn Hughes.

Sagittaria montevidensis

Aztec arrowhead

Height: 2'

Zone: 3

Blooms: Summer

Aspect: Sun

Photo by Eamonn Hughes.

Saururus cernuus

Lizard tail

Height: 2'

Zone: 4

Blooms: Summer

Aspect: Sun

Photo by Eamonn Hughes.

Scirpus zebrinus

Zebra rush

Height: 5'

Zone: 3

Blooms: Summer

Aspect: Part shade

Photo by Gordon T. Ledbetter.

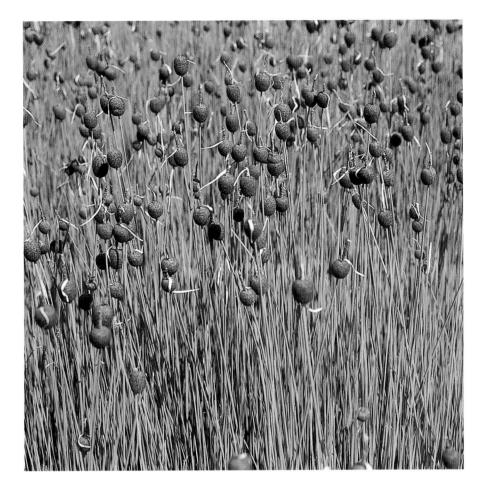

Typha minima

Miniature cattail

Height: 2'

Zone: 3

Blooms: Summer

Aspect: Sun

Photo by Eamonn Hughes.

Menyanthes trifoliata

Bog bean

Height: 1'

Zone: 5

Blooms: Summer

Aspect: Part shade

Photo by Eamonn Hughes.

Cotton grass (Eriophorum angustifolium) growing along this stream has begun to grow out into the courseway. The water flow eventually will be disrupted if the plants are not routinely thinned. Photo by Eamonn Hughes.

Other Plants for the Stream Garden

Acorus calamus
Sweetflag
Height: 1-4'
Zone: 4
Blooms: Summer
Aspect: Sun

Acorus gramineus 'Variegata'
Variegated dwarf sweetflag
Height: 9"
Zone: 7
Blooms: Spring-Summer
Aspect: Sun

Cardamine cordifolia
Heartleaved bittercress
Height: 4-32"
Zone: 5
Blooms: Early Summer
Aspect: Shade to sun

Carex obnupta
Slough sedge
Height: 2'
Zone: 4
Blooms: Summer
Aspect: Sun

Echinodorus cordifolia
Radican sword
Height: 2'
Zone: 6
Blooms: Summer
Aspect: Part shade

Eriophorum angustifolium
Cotton grass
Zone: 4
Blooms: Summer
Aspect: Sun

Hydrocotyle umbellata
Pennywort
height: 1'
Zone: 5
Blooms: Summer
Aspect: Sun

Iris 'Black Gamecock'
Black gamecock iris
Height: 18"
Zone: 5
Blooms: Spring
Aspect: Part shade

Iris fulva
Red iris
Height: 1'
Zone: 5
Blooms: Spring
Aspect: Part shade

Juncus effusus

Soft rush

Height: 2'

Zone: 3

Blooms: Summer

Aspect: Sun

Juncus ensifolius

Dagger leaf rush

Height: 1'

Zone: 3

Blooms: Summer

Aspect: Sun

Juncus patens

Blue Spreading rush

Height: 18"

Zone: 3

Blooms: Summer

Aspect: Sun

Lysimmachia nummularia

Creeping jenny

Height: creeper

Zone: 4

Blooms: Summer

Aspect: Part shade

**Lysimmachia nummularia
'Aurea'**

Yellow-leafed creeping jenny

Height: creeper

Zone: 4

Blooms: Summer

Aspect: Sun

Nasturtium officinale

Watercress

Height: creeper

Zone: 6

Blooms: Spring-Summer

Aspect: Part shade

(see also *Cardamine cordifolia*)

Ranunculus flammula

Small Creeping spearwort

Height: 6"

Zone: 3

Blooms: Spring-Summer

Aspect: Sun

Typha laxmanii

Graceful cattail

Height: 4'

Blooms: Summer

Aspect: Sun

CONVERTING TO METRIC

To Convert	Multiply by	To Obtain
inches	2.54	centimeters
inches	25.4	millimeters
feet	30	centimeters
pounds	0.45	kilograms
U.S. gallons	3.8	liters

Fahrenheit to Celsius: Subtract 32, multiply by 5, divide by 9.

ACKNOWLEDGMENTS

Special thanks to Marsha Alley; Atlanta builder Cla Allgood; Texas landscaper Dave Artz; Scott Bates of Grass Roots Nursery, in New Boston, Michigan; Carol Christensen; Joe Cook; Marilyn Cook, for drawings; Peter Davidson, of Zen Water Gardens, in Montecito, California; Lee Dreyfuss; Ron Everhart; Florentine Craftsmen; Charles A. Henne; Oliver Jackson; Greg Jones; Irelands's international water feature designer Gordon T. Ledbetter; Little Giant Pump Corporation; Bill Marocco; Greg Maxwell, of Maxwell Tree Experts, in Fort Wayne, Indiana; Deb Moak; Anita Nelson, of Nelson Water Gardens, in Katy, Texas; Oase Pumps; Carole Taylor Reimer; Rena Corporation, now a division of Aquarium Pharmaceuticals; Bob Romar and Maryland Aquatic Nurseries; Richard Sacher, of American Aquatic Gardens, in New Orleans; Richard Schmitz; T.J. Smith; Steve Stroupe, of Davis Creek Nursery, in McCalla, Alabama; and Jim Sullivan, of Living Fountains, in Sedona, Arizona.

INDEX

(Boldface page numbers denote plants.)

A

acorus calamus, **124**

acorus gramineus 'variegata,' **124**

atmosphere, 13–14

B

back mortaring, 31

bio-filter systems, 46

birds, 46–47

brick, 20

building supplies, computing quantities of, 20

butomus umbellatus, **113**

C

calla palustris, **114**

caltha palustris, **114–115**

cardamine cordifolia, **124**

carex obnupta, **124**

carved construction, 42

cement, 20

centrifugal pumps, 76

cobbles, 20

color wheel, 94

concrete, 20, 28, 67

contractors, 21

cost, project, 14, 17

crater rock, 20

cyperus alternifolius, **115**

D

datum peg, 24, 25

depth, of water, 18

design layout, 14–17

E

echinodorus cordifolia, **124**

electrical service, 65

eleocharis palustris, **116**

EPDM adhesive, 38, 51, 52

eriophorum angustifolium, **124**

European fountain designs, 107–108

excavation, 26–28

for streambed, 63–64, 66–67

for waterfalls, 38

external pumps, 76

F

featherock boulders, 20

filters, pump, 76, 81

filtration, vegetative, 45–46

flagstone, 20

formed framework construction, 42–43, 54–55

fountains

bell, 85, 86

European designs, 107–108

foaming head, 85, 86

kits, 83–84

large, 85, 90, 95

maintenance of, 106–107

plumbed statuary, 95–99

public, 109–112

pumps for. *See* Pumps

Rena, 88–89

spray, 85, 86

tiered, 85

types of, 85–87

wall, 100–102

G

granite, 20

ground cover aggregates, 20

ground settling, 38–39

gunnite rock, 54

H

hardcore, 20

hidden reservoir stream, 72

hose or water level, 24–25, 26

houttuynia cordata, **116, 117**

hydrocotyle umbellata, **124**

I

installation

determining levels, 23–26

excavation, 26–28

liner, setting of, 28

mixing mortar for, 28–29

moving rocks for, 30

setting rocks for, 31

iris 'black gamecock,' **124**

iris fulva, **124**

iris pseudacorus, **117**

iris versicolor, **118**

J

juncus effusus, **125**

juncus ensifolius, **125**

juncus patens, 70, **125**

L

landscape architects, 21

levels

determining, 23–26

section, establishing, 27

of streambed, 64

lights, underwater, 94

limestone, crushed, 20

line level, 25

liner

selection, 17

setting, 28

size requirements, 18

streambed, 64–65, 67

for waterfalls, 35, 38

Little Giant pumps, 90, 91, 94

lysimmachia nummularia, **125**

M

marble boulders, 20

materials, required, 21

menyanthes trifoliata, **123**

millstones, 106

mimulus guttatus, **118**

mortar, 20